AF255898

Beyond the Dirt Road

Becky Stoker Kyle

To James

Preface

The impetus for this book came at an unexpected time. After Hurricane Harvey destroyed much of the Gulf Coast, we sat for days waiting to see if our home would be inundated by water. We were blessed to be spared this horrible misfortune. Many of our friends and neighbors were not so fortunate. On one of these days, I found myself staring out of my office window, thinking about the words that had so often cluttered my mind. It was at this moment that I made the decision to put these words into a book, which hopefully, will preserve the things in my life that history will soon forget. My children and grandchildren should know that I did this for them. After I am gone, I pray that on occasion, they will take a moment to revisit a page or two. Perhaps, this will help them remember me and how much I loved them. I thank God for them every day.

If, in our fifty-three years together, I have failed to convey to James how much I love and appreciate him, it is my hope that this book will make amends. He has been my rock and my strength.

Many people have helped and encouraged me throughout this endeavor. I am especially grateful to Gloria Durr Bryant, who allowed me to share her life in a most touching way. Evelyn Brandenburg, my friend and hairdresser, proved to be an invaluable source as she shared her writing experience with me. My editor, Carol Dennis, reminded me that my English background had faded into oblivion. Cynthia McAdams removed any worry about publishing details. Her knowledge and confidence were very reassuring. My dear friend, Jean Sanders, offered support and encouragement as only she can.

My many friends should know they have been an inspiration to me at every turn. I appreciate and value each and every one of you. I truly hope that you enjoy *Beyond the Dirt Road*.

1

The Early Years

I have struggled with the idea of writing a book for several years. At 75, it is now or never. It is unclear to me whether or not I have anything of worth to say. We will see. I was born in 1942 in Many, Louisiana. At this time, my Dad was principal at a small school in a very rural area of Sabine Parish, Louisiana. This community was known as Toro, or Pisgah, Louisiana. Today, much of this area is under Toledo Bend Lake. One has only to read my Dad's book, *Telling It Like It Was* to understand how hard life was for my parents at Toro. They spent much of the war years there, enduring the maneuvers when General Patton was conducting war games in preparation for his European Campaign. They lived in what was known in those days as a teacher's cottage. I might add that as newlyweds, this was along with three old maid teachers. Eventually, they moved to a small shotgun house near the school yard. No running water inside; therefore, no inside toilets. Cooking was done on a wood stove.

These are the conditions into which I was born. Not exactly the Waldorf. My Father later told me that he did not think the old maid teachers would take kindly to a crying baby, thus the move to the little house.

My Mother came from a very poor family and my Father from what was at one time, a prosperous farming family. During the depression, my Grandfather was losing the farm to unpaid taxes. My Dad worked summers to save it. My husband and I own the farm today.

We moved to a small town called Noble, Louisiana, when I was two. Dad was principal of Noble school for one year. In 1944, we moved to another small town, Pleasant Hill. It is here where I spent the formative years of my life. We do not know to this day why Dad was not called into the service. He volunteered, took the physical and never got called. When I left for college, my parents still lived in this little town.

It is here that my story really begins. My memories of growing up in this small town are real and vivid. I remember little or nothing of my life before moving to what we often call "pea hill". We lived in a big old house on the edge of the school yard. It was not fancy, but I remember it as being warm and comfortable. This was my home until my senior year in high school.

My first memory of my new life is simple. I remember standing at the gate in our back yard, looking up at the school house, waiting for Mother and Daddy to come home. A picture exists showing me leaning over our dog Snuffy, looking toward the school. There was a little trail leading from the house to the front door of the school. It strikes me today how beautiful the old school building was. Made of red brick, covered with ivy, it reminds one of the Ivy League buildings up East. Eventually, it was torn down and replaced with a more modern facility.

Until I reached school age, I was looked after by two wonderful black women, Aunt Ollie and Aunt Coe. To this day, I do not know what their last names were. Aunt Coe did the washing outside in a big black pot over an open fire. Aunt Ollie cleaned

Baby Becky – 6 months

Daddy, Becky and Mama on steps of Pleasant Hill School

and supervised me, such as it was. When Aunt Coe washed, I was always right under her feet. She taught me to say a few things that were not exactly appropriate for a three year old. One day, she decided to teach me to preach, accompanied by all the antics of her black minister. She would have me stomp around the yard, waving my arms and shouting warnings about the wrath of God. When Mother and Daddy came home from school, I was more than happy to demonstrate my new-found talent. Needless-to-say, they were not too happy with their three year old, or for that matter, Aunt Coe. This did not stop me when they were out of sight. I loved to preach to Aunt Coe when she was washing. One day, she had spread the coals out farther than usual. I was marching around, not paying attention when all of a sudden I stepped on the hot coals. Large blisters appeared on the bottom of both of my feet. Daddy, or someone, carried me around for days. Today, I would have been taken to the emergency room.

Aunt Ollie was a gentle soul. My favorite time was her ironing days. These were the days that I got to hear her snake stories. I would sit on the bed while she ironed and listen intently to the biggest whoppers that Aunt Ollie could conjure up. The story that I have carried to this day is so farfetched that it seems impossible that even a three year old would believe it. According to Aunt Ollie, one day she went for a walk in the woods in her native state of South Carolina. She sat on a log to rest. The log started crawling off. That's how big snakes are in South Carolina. Over the years, every time I sit on a log, I think of Aunt Ollie. If there is a moral to this story, I assume it to be watch where you sit!

I loved Aunt Ollie and Aunt Coe. They did not exactly provide an environment filled with intellectual stimulation; however, they loved me and cared for me the best that they knew how. Daddy took me to see them for many years after they were unable to work.

2

School Days

I started school in 1948. My first grade teacher was Mrs. Johnson. She was a beautiful lady who always smelled so good. I do not remember how many kids were in my first grade class. When we graduated twelve years later, there were eighteen of us. Basically, we went to school together for the entire twelve years. A few kids would come and go. Mostly, it was the same bunch, in the same class, for all of those years. First grade must have gone pretty well. I remember, my classmate, Kenneth cried for the first few weeks. I guess he did not want to go to school. He was so cute with his little khaki pants and suspenders. I remember feeling sorry for him. At six, I did not understand why Kenneth had to go to school if he did not want to. Mrs. Johnson left after our first grade year to marry a rich jeweler from Texarkana.

Mrs. Tarbox was my second grade teacher. She taught us through her wonderful lessons that there was a bigger world out there. Through simple second grade activities, we explored other cultures and countries. I remember being fascinated by a unit on eskimos, where we constructed igloos using paste and paper. More than anything else, Mrs. Tarbox exposed us to an exciting and interesting world. Fortunately, in the years to come, many of us found and explored that world. Mrs. Tarbox was fun, but she did not put up with foolishness out of us. The dreaded fear was that we would be sent into the hall. Daddy walked the halls. If he saw anyone in the hall, boy, were they in trouble! I knew full well that

I had better not be found in the hall. Mr. Tarbox always brought Mrs. Tarbox to and from school. They had an old car that would be a true antique today. I have often wondered what happened to that car.

Mrs. Jackson taught third grade. She always had this strange smell about her. One day, being a typical third grader, I asked her why she always smelled funny. Not such a polite thing to do. Her response was wonderful. She told me that she had a skin problem and used a cream called Noxzema to help it. Mrs. Jackson also added that she was glad that I asked. This pleased me because I felt that I had made her feel good by asking. I am sure that she wanted to send me into the hall to receive the wrath of Daddy. The thing I remember most about third grade is the book *Children of the Covered Wagon*. Mrs. Jackson would read a chapter to us each day. We waited, not too patiently, for her to begin reading. It is a wonderful book which chronicled the hardships faced by our early settlers as they traveled west. I doubt if it is even on library shelves today. This simple story gave me a prospective on the hardships that our ancestors endured.

Becky – 2nd grade

As I view our country today, I am angered that these sacrifices are not recognized, especially by many of our younger generation. In fact, it scares me to death that so many people on the streets of America know nothing about our history. It mortifies me when street reporters cannot get basic answers from ordinary citizens about our leaders and our past. We simply cannot take our freedom for granted. I am reminded again what this book is about. It is about how growing up in a small town and rural area can influence one's work ethics and values. Above all, it is about how my classmates found opportunity and eventually that larger world that Mrs. Tarbox revealed to us. It is also about how I personally found that larger world.

Miss Dowell, my fourth grade teacher, was Mrs. Jackson's sister. They rode to school together because they lived in the country near each other. For some unknown reason, my hormones started bumping in fourth grade. Or maybe a bad gene popped out. I spent a good deal of time in the cloak room. The cloak room was a long room where we kept our coats, boots and lunches. By fourth grade, Daddy had built a school lunchroom. I believe Mrs. Dowell sent me to the cloak room because she did not want Daddy to find me in the hall and kill me. I mentioned the lunchroom because it resulted in a trip to the cloak room one day. We often had turnip greens for lunch. They were always stringy. I found one string on my tray that must have been a foot long. At the time, it seemed fine to hold the green string way above my head and feed it into my mouth. Mrs. Dowell did not think it was funny, so I got sent to the cloak room when we returned to class. At least, the kids laughed at my antics.

My fifth grade year was uneventful. Miss Hinds was very sweet and kind. My memories of anything in particular are vague. I guess my hormone bumps stopped. Sixth grade with Mrs. Chase was also a good year. I recall having a horrible rash on both of my sides. The doctor gave me medication that put me to sleep. I remember going to sleep in class. Mrs. Chase would kindly wake me up. I am afraid that I was not so kind to my students who went to sleep in class years later.

Mrs. Freeman was my seventh grade teacher. I remember her as an excellent teacher. I cannot for the life of me recall my eighth grade year. Evidently, I had several teachers come and go during the year. High school years that followed had a profound effect on my personality. These years probably affected the way that I faced life in the days and years to come.

3

Life at Home

Life at home for me was good. When I was in elementary school, Daddy moved a lady next door to us with the idea that she would help take care of me. Mother and Daddy were so busy working and going to meetings here and there that I was often in need of someone to keep me, at times over night. Ma Rains became this person for many years to come. Daddy had her little house moved next door to us. She was my second mother and grandmother. I spent more time at her house than at ours. She made the best and biggest biscuits which she served with a thick piece of warm fatback. Ma did not have much, but she made the best of it. People would give her wild game which she would cook to perfection. Her "coon and taters" was the best wild game that I've ever eaten. She fried sweet potatoes with the raccoon, probably in pure lard.

As an adult, I could be adventurous. I have also eaten rattlesnake, alligator and mountain oysters. During the summer, Ma and Daddy would garden together in the big space behind our house. We were never in need of fresh or frozen produce. Mother and Ma put up tons of food during the gardening season.

Along with the good came the bad. Daddy was involved in educational activities all over the state. He was gone a lot, which was hard on Mother. Many days she worked at school until dark. Ma was always there. My parents were very concerned with their image in our little town. I was told, at least once a day, that I should never do anything to tarnish our name. I interpreted this to mean that Daddy could get fired if I did something wrong. This is a large burden for a child to bear and it followed me for years. I worried far too long about what people thought. Many of my high school accomplishments were characterized by my classmates as the result of being the principal's daughter. Every time someone said this to me – and believe me, kids did say that to me – it hurt my feelings.

Becky and her bull

There were times when I began to doubt my own abilities. I hid my insecurities well because I believe some of my classmates saw me as aloof and unfriendly. I was being pressured by my parents to excel in everything that I did. Some of these things made me uncomfortable, especially becoming a cheerleader. I tried out and was selected to be an alternate. I hated every time we took the floor to cheer. That was way outside of my comfort zone.

My school years were busy. I was active in 4H. Daddy decided that I needed to raise two calves and show them at the state livestock show. I much preferred to continue my award-winning insect collection. To this day, I can identify any common insect by order and a common name. Folks didn't stop me on the street to ask me to do this; however, it did impress my future students. Anyway, back to the calves. I raised two Hereford calves, one a bull and the other a heifer, to show in Baton Rouge. The bull was so tame that I rode it around like a horse. The heifer was as wild as the bull was tame. She had a propensity for escaping the small pasture behind our house. Daddy would chase her down and return her to her little pasture. Things came to a head one day when she escaped and got into Miss Annie Glass's collard patch. She apparently cleaned it out. When we finally got to Baton Rouge, she dragged me around the arena about six times while I was trying to show her. Needless to say, we did not do well. If I remember correctly, my bull won sixth place. I have gotten to know a few heifers in my seventy-five years. None were as wild as this one.

I was a fairly good athlete in high school. The only sport for girls was softball. I pitched and played right field. I was a pretty good pitcher until my horse Vic threw me off and hurt my arm. I did not tell Daddy because I was afraid he would sell Vic. Several years later, I found out that my arm was broken and never set. I did not throw a windup pitch the way girls do today. I just pitched the ball. Christine Durr was our catcher. She saved many pitches from going God knows where. Christine was some athlete. I did not tell Daddy about my arm until he was ninety years old. I figured that he was too old to spank me by this time.

4

My Schoolmates

Several miles from town, way out in the country, the Durr family lived in what today would be called poverty. Back then, they were simply poor. Of the many students he mentored, Christine Durr was always one of daddy's favorites. The Durr kids were always sweet, well- behaved, and attentive to their school work. Christine, the softball catcher, was a tough tomboy. No one dared mess with her because they knew that she would win. Her sister Gloria Faye was in my class. Christine was a year or two younger. Gloria Faye was always kind to me in high school, and I pray that I was kind to her. I never remember her getting angry or upset. Christine and I were always buddies, probably because I was a tomboy, too. She undoubtedly got tired of chasing my wild pitches all over the place.

Several years ago, I received a call from Fannie Gates, another of my classmates. Some of my classmates were organizing a class reunion at Dallas Britt's home. I will always be grateful to Dallas because I felt that he took up for me during those high school years. It was a struggle for me to make up my mind to go as I still felt some sting from those early years. My husband encouraged me to go, so I did. I had not been back to Pleasant Hill since our wedding day. When we arrived at Dallas's house, almost everyone was there. The group greeted me warmly and we begin to play the "can you recognize me game." I did well with everyone, with the exception of Dallas and one female classmate. Dallas had lost the extra weight he carried in high school. He became a nice-looking guy. I simply would never have recognized him if he had not identified himself. The female stumped me. Who was this attractive, well-dressed woman? She realized that I was at a stalemate so she said, "I'm Gloria Faye Durr."

It is my belief that Gloria Faye and I bonded that day. I have great admiration for what she has achieved. At the reunion we spent some one-on-one time with each other. I had no idea what had happened to her after high school. She explained that after graduation, she went to work for Adam's Extract Company in Austin, Texas. Gloria Faye, the little girl from Pleasant Hill, became Vice-President of this major company. After recovering from this wonderful revelation, I listened to Gloria relate a story which has stayed with me and touched me over the years.

She told me that she was on a business trip to New York City, accompanied by her husband. They were having lunch at Tavern on the Green when tears began to run down her cheeks. Her concerned husband asked why she was crying. She responded, "I never dreamed that a little girl who lived down a long dirt road would be looking out over Central Park while having lunch at Tavern on the Green." I'm thinking, "You, my friend, have moved beyond that dirt road." It is important to add here that Gloria's husband Jackie is a hero of the Viet Nam War. He was inducted into the Louisiana Tech Hall of Fame as a result of this and his other accomplishments. Louisiana Tech is my alma mater. Gloria and I have stayed in touch since the reunion. Not as much or as often as I would like because we are both very busy ladies.

I have one more Gloria story to tell. For twenty plus years, Lloyd has taken care of our farm. He lives two miles up the road from our old home and about twenty miles from Natchitoches where Gloria lives. He shares a house with his brother and elderly mother, and they often shop at the Walmart in Natchitoches. Gloria called me a few months ago. "I've got to tell you this story," she told me. It seems that Gloria was in Walmart in the detergent area, when she noticed an elderly woman with two older men looking for something. Being the gracious lady that she is, she asked them if she could help. They explained that they had a new washing machine and needed a special kind of washing powder. Since, they were having a time locating the detergent, Gloria found it for them and then struck up a conversation. She asked where they

Lloyd and Tyler on the four-wheeler

lived. They told her Ft. Jessup, which is the community where our farm is located. Gloria then asked Lloyd what he did. After some hesitation, Lloyd replied that he worked for a rich old lady in Ft. Jessup. Gloria told me, "I immediately knew they were talking about you." First of all, there are not many people in Fort Jessup, so that was a clue. I do not know why the rich old lady description was a clue. Remember that I taught school for thirty-eight years. By the way, I do not consider myself old. At any rate, Gloria and I had a big laugh over this one.

It turned out that I really enjoyed the reunion and seeing my old classmates. While there, I admired a steel picnic bench that Dallas had in his yard. "Would you like to have one?" he asked me. I said, "Yes, but only if you will let me pay for it." Dallas had one made for us and delivered it to the farm. It now sits at our ranch in Junction, Texas. At one point, I went into the house where Dallas's wife Cindy was taking care of the massive amount of food. "You know that Dallas had a big crush on you in high school," she said. I responded, "Cindy, I'm very flattered." This truly came from my heart. I am very saddened that Dallas passed away much too early.

Jesse Bridges came to the reunion. He was salutatorian and I was valedictorian. It seems that we were always in competition with each other. By the time the reunion came along, Jesse was very sick. He had attended Louisiana Tech on a basketball scholarship. My friend Sue Hardee, Jesse, and I, all attended Louisiana Tech. Sue did not attend the reunion; however, I have seen her a few times over the years. She was kind enough to attend the visitations when my parents passed away. When Daddy was honored by the Sabine Parish Hall of Fame, I saw her then. The reunion gave Jesse and I a chance to visit with each other after all of those years. We walked around Dallas's yard arm in arm. He was so weak that he needed me to steady him. Any hard feelings were mended in those moments. I told him that I had great respect for him and that he had pushed me to be better at every turn. I am grateful that I had those few moments with him. He passed away not too long after this meeting.

Patsy Free was one of my best friends in high school. She lived in the country with her grandmother, who was a wonderful lady. Patsy spent many nights with me. We both took piano lessons from Miss Bessie Payne. At one recital, Miss Payne saddled Patsy and me with a duet. I am sure that Patsy thought about pushing me off the piano bench on more than one practice session. I took piano for eleven years and miss being able to play because of a compression in my arm which affected my fingers. When Miss Bessie would get really aggravated with me, she would say: "Becky, when you are seventy, you will not be able to play softball, but you can play the piano." How right she was!

I remember that I would put the clock by the piano, so that I would not practice a minute too long. After all, the boys were waiting for me at the softball field right by our house. At the time, I thought they were waiting for me. Not so. Daddy kept the baseball and softball equipment on our back porch. When I came to the field, I brought the equipment bag.

Miss Payne always took us to the Music Festival at Northwestern University in Natchitoches. I always waited until the last minute to memorize my Bach Invention; whereas, Patsy was always ready. Maybe that is why she usually rated Superior and I was downgraded to Excellent. I recall one festival in particular. In the comment section, after I had played my Bach Invention, the judge wrote: "Seems to be a very musical child. This is the first time I have seen a beat put in Bach." Our senior year, Patsy was voted Most Likely To Succeed. Jesse was Best Dressed, and I was Most

Athletic. After high school, Patsy got her degree and became a teacher. I have no doubt that she was a very good one.

Fannie Gates and Faye Walker were also my friends. I can still picture Fannie standing by the radiator before class in the mornings. She often ate a box of pretzel sticks. Not the best nutrition for breakfast, but it suited Fannie. Faye was always very kind and sweet. She hosted another class reunion more recently. I was unable to attend because of my multiple health problems. Gloria told me that everyone had a good time.

Dale Robinson and Pearl Moore, a quiet, sweet girl, are two

Miss Payne's music students

of our other deceased classmates. When we could find a place to dance, Dale was always popular because he was a good dancer. I found Dale's inscription in my yearbook. He wrote about parties at my house and referred to them as wild. I remember parties where we danced. I certainly do not remember them being wild. Not at my daddy's house! We were not allowed to have school dances in our little Baptist town. We had to be content with our yearly junior-senior banquet. It was always lovely because of the talents of my hard- working mother. Daddy gave my graduation party at the Ft. Jessup Park museum. He bused the entire class of eighteen to Ft. Jessup, which was twenty plus miles from Pleasant Hill. Of course, the bus was a school bus. We were out of town so we were allowed to dance. Boy, did we dance!

Sissy Taylor, also at the reunion, was Most Beautiful in the yearbook favorites section. Her younger brother James was voted Most Handsome. Donald Ray, Sissy's older brother, was a year older than I was. We were friends because he was always around Mother and Daddy. They loved him and constantly worked with him on different endeavors. My freshman year at Tech, I invited

Donald Ray to my sorority spring formal. He came all the way from Baton Rouge to take me. At that time, he was in pre-med at LSU. When he graduated from medical school, he came back to his home turf to practice. Donald Ray and I were friends, and I was unwilling to rescind my invitation to him. He never knew that on that spring formal night, I was already dating my future husband.

5

Other Influences

Two of my favorite high school teachers were Mrs. Fisher and Mrs. Emmons. Mrs. Fisher taught typing and math. She also worked for Daddy in the office during her off-period. That is, if she had an off-period. Mrs. Emmons taught home economics, and I must have been her worst nightmare. Our senior year, we were required to make a dress. With Mrs. Emmons' help, I finished the dress down to the hemming. While we were working on the hem, she came around to observe everyone. Unknowingly, I had sewed the dress I was making to the dress that I was wearing. When I held the hem up for her to see, I pulled my dress almost over my head. I never wore that dress. To this day, I have trouble sewing on a button.

I cannot leave my formative years without making mention of the influence of the church in my life. Daddy was a deacon in the Pleasant Hill First Baptist Church. We went every time the doors opened. When we got our first TV, I begged to stay home on Sunday nights. Of course, this went over like a lead balloon. I remember thinking, "One day, when I am old, I will not go unless I want to." Regretfully, for many years, James and I were not very faithful church goers. Regardless, I am convinced that it was here in this small church that I learned the core values that I have carried through all of my adult life. Five years after graduating from high school, I married my husband in this church. Brother Cecil Sally, who baptized me when I was twelve, married us.

6

Louisiana Tech

As I grew older, I came to realize that these early years were good years. I now know that most of my demons were of my own making and that the good things outweighed the bad. In some ways, my life changed after I left home. I began to experience that other world Mrs. Tarbox, my second grade teacher, exposed me to. This journey began at Louisiana Tech. Although it was only ninety miles from Pleasant Hill, it was a world away for me.

Upon arrival at Tech, I was assigned to live in Harper Hall. It was the oldest dorm on campus and could easily be characterized as a dump. The bathrooms and showers were at the other end of the hall from my room. I would compare the distance to a football field's length. As freshmen, we had to wear stupid green beanies. If we forgot to wear them, and were caught by an upperclassman, we had to kneel and sing the silly song, "I am a lowly freshman." I got really good at singing this little classic.

I was elected vice-president of the dorm. With this came the responsibility of becoming head of the judiciary council. In other words, I held court once a week. Shortly after the semester began, my first test of character occurred. Since I did not know anyone to room with, I was assigned a roommate. She seemed nice enough and we got along fine. For the life of me, I cannot remember her name. One Saturday night, she came in drunk as a skunk. Not only was she drunk, she paraded down the hall to the bathroom, stumbling and singing. Everyone saw her and everyone looked at me with that "What are you going to do?" look. I was terrified; however, I swallowed hard and carted her off to the dorm mother's quarters. For me, that was a terribly difficult thing to do. For the remainder of the semester, she was not allowed to leave the dorm except for class. She must have realized that I did the only thing that I could do because we had a cordial relationship the rest of the semester. My, how things have changed! The only legal thing that couples could do on campus in 1960 was hold hands. Today, that's almost a joke. Everything occurs on campus these days, even non-consensual sex. It turns out, they really were the good old days.

7

Daddy

When I left for Tech, Daddy set me up with a checking account at our small town bank. He did not realize that my knowledge of finance was zero at best. When I attended high school, there was a room that was used for afternoon break. It contained a coke machine and a small candy store. It was here that I got my experience in finance. This consisted of begging Daddy for six cents for a coke, which, after much pleading, he would give me. Naturally, Mother worked in the candy store along with her other umpteen responsibilities. She was school librarian in her spare time. Thankfully, she would feel sorry for me and give me something from the store. Most of the time, it was a box of Fannie's pretzels.

I loved my checking account. I could go over to Anderson's Grocery Store and buy anything I wanted, or at least I thought so. I also purchased important things from the college bookstore. Stuffed bull dogs by the dozen adorned my dorm room. Shortly, after the beginning of the second semester, I got a call from Daddy. He was livid! Mr. Freeman, at the bank had called. "Becky is bouncing checks all over Ruston." Daddy drove to Ruston the next day and gave me a lesson in finance. Thank goodness, the bank paid all of the checks. Daddy would have sent me all over Ruston to pick up those checks and apologize.

By now, it should be clear that my Dad was a special force in my life. I was the boy he never had, and I think he tried to make me into one. After Daddy came to Lake Jackson to be with us, we spent hours at the nursing home visiting and reminiscing. I went to see him every day and sometimes twice. James would always come by after work if he was not out of town on business. One evening in 2003, Daddy became very ill. The nursing home informed me that he was probably not going to pull through this one. After much prayer and anguish, I made the decision to let him go peacefully. For the three days that he lay unaware of his surroundings, I tried to whisper in his ear that LSU had won the National Championship. I hope that he heard me. I stayed by his side for the entire three days. Finally, the hospice nurse said, "You have to go home and get some rest." James insisted and we went home. As we stepped into the house, the telephone was ringing. Daddy was gone. I will always believe that he waited until I left to go. Daddy never really got over Mother's death, and I am very sure that he could not wait to see her again.

Mother died in 1995, after undergoing her second mitral valve replacement. Her little body was so worn out that she was unable to survive the surgery at eighty-three. The doctors told us that it was unlikely that she would pull through. Daddy was so distraught that he could not bear to see her. It was left to me to visit her in intensive care during every visitation. I stayed in Baton Rouge for six weeks on a temporary leave from my teaching position. I held her hand as she passed away. My heart broke into a thousand pieces. Being an only child is not always easy.

Since I was a little kid, I have loved to fish. If Daddy and I could slip off, we would go out to one of the local farm ponds to fish. The meaning of "slip off" is if we could get away from school before Mother caught us. We had an old 1949 truck which I started driving when I was ten. Daddy would come by my last period class and call me out of the room. He would instruct me to run home, get the old truck loaded, and pick him up at the end of the building. We had this maneuver down pat. Seldom, did we get caught. Mother got her revenge on one of these escapes. It dawned on me that Daddy was fishing ahead of me, so I proceeded to run behind him to get ahead. Much to my dismay, he cast his lure just as I ran behind him. I ended up with a big Hula Popper embedded in my shoulder. I never saw my dad so rattled. When he realized how bad it was, he lost it. I think it was at this moment that I knew how much he loved me. We jumped in the old truck and headed for the clinic. Daddy cried all the way to town. While crying, he kept muttering. "God, please let Dr. Prothro be at the clinic. Honey, I'm so sorry. Mama's gonna kill me." Dr. Prothro and his nurse Nelwyn Jacobs were still there. The old plug was so deeply embedded, the doctor ended up cutting it out. I do not remember how old I was when this happened, but to this day, I still fresh water fish with a Hula Popper.

8

Meeting James

The second semester started with me carrying a full load, including qualitative analysis chemistry. The lab was two days a week and three hours long. In this lab, I met the man who became my husband and continues to be the love of my life. We were assigned a lab desk full of supplies. One of these supplies was an ugly, black acid- resistant apron. During the first lab session, I could not get my apron tied in the back. I looked around for help and for the first time noticed that the guy next to me was tall, handsome and pleasant looking. He seemed to know what was going on. I asked him if he would please tie my lab apron and he did. We introduced ourselves, and I found out that he was majoring in chemical engineering. I started to Tech in pre-dentistry. To this day, I have no idea why because I now know that I did not want to spend my life looking in people's mouths, and adjusting their dentures.

After this first lab session, James would spar with my friend Keith Colvin for a seat next to me during the morning lecture. Keith and I met at a National Science Foundation Institute which we attended the summer between our junior and senior years in high school. Keith became a physician, and I have lost contact with him over the years. Most days, it was James on one side and Keith on the other. I kept wondering if James would ask me out on a date. Finally, one day he asked me if I would like to go out for a coke after lab. I said yes, but that I could not go until the next afternoon because I had a sorority meeting. I pledged Alpha

Chi Omega, and James pledged Pi Kappa Alpha. We did not have a lab that afternoon, so this was a better time. At least, it should have been. I forgot the date and was over at the infirmary visiting a sorority sister. Miss Gillenwaters, the infirmary nurse, came to get me. She told me that a young man was waiting outside for me. Then, I remembered. In my mind, I can still see that picture today. James was standing with his foot against the wall with a big smile on his face. He was wearing the most beautiful blue sweater. My first thought was, "How could I have forgotten this?" I apologized, which he took in stride, and we left for the little Dairy Delight on the edge of campus. I ordered a coke. He came back with one coke. I found out later he only had enough money for one twenty-five cent coke.

Mrs. Gillenwaters was not finished with us. During our junior year, when James was in the infirmary with a bad cold, she caught us kissing. She was content to give us a lecture on passing germs around. Thank heavens! We could have gotten in grave trouble for that "public display of affection."

Becky and James at the AXΩ spring party

Soon after the coke date, we were together every free moment. We studied for our chemistry tests together in the dorm lobby. James would get upset with me for not concentrating. I was concentrating all right, but on the wrong thing. My grades went down, and in rides Daddy on a white horse. He arranged with Dean Condra for me to study on the third floor of Harper. I was the only one up there most of the time. The sorority suites were also on the third floor; however, they were usually empty. The next semester, I changed my major to English and biology education. I quickly went from Daddy's list to the Dean's list. James was in class and engineering labs all day. This little arrangement was good for both of us.

With the change in my major, college became a new game. I

AXΩ Spring Formal

was having the time of my life, while enjoying the success that I was experiencing in my classes. The sorority and fraternity events were always fun. I finally got to dance. James had two left feet and still does. This never stopped us from having a good time. His parents paid to send him to Arthur Murray Dance Studio in Monroe. It was wasted money.

After our sophomore year, it was apparent that we were serious. Our attraction for each other was strong and remains so to this day. We spent many weekends with our parents, usually studying or relaxing. James's dad was a mess. He raised domestic rabbits which I later learned tasted better than chicken. I told him that I would never eat rabbit. At the time, I did not relate this to the "coon and taters" that I ate at Ma Rains' house. Mr. Kyle decided that I would eat rabbit. Like his son, he was a great cook. He fixed a chicken salad, substituting the rabbit for the chicken. James and I went to Monroe for the weekend, and I had my first bite of the salad. It was delicious. I went on and on about it. All the while, James and his dad were enjoying every minute of this little prank. I learned about this episode long after we were married.

We got engaged when we were seniors. James asked Daddy for permission and he gave it. When the engagement ring was purchased, James was making seventy-five cents an hour grading papers for one of the engineering professors. Over the years Daddy became very fond of my husband. Actually, James became the son that he never had. Daddy always called him Jim as do most of our friends. I remain the only person who calls him James. He will always be my James.

9

Starting Work

I graduated a semester before James did since engineering required more hours than a regular four-year degree. We planned to get married in November, after he graduated in August. We decided that I should go to work and try to save some money. That was a joke. I was offered a job with Shell Oil Company in New Orleans because of my unusual science and English background. The position was engineering writer. I was also one of two Tech graduates who were offered a teaching position in Brazosport Independent School District in Freeport, Texas. The teaching job was at Lake Jackson Junior High in Lake Jackson. The other person offered a job was Martha Vining. Her future husband Roy was James fraternity brother at Tech. Martha accepted the job in Lake Jackson because Roy, also an engineer, had accepted a job at Dow Chemical. Roy eventually became mayor of Lake Jackson. Martha and I have been friends for a long time. I decided to take this job for another reason. This was the highest paying district in Texas at the time, a big whopping five thousand forty a year. After graduation, Mother and Daddy bought me a 1963 Super Sports Chevy. It was a fine car, and I wish that we had it today. I had to report for the January semester. I and the Chevy took off to Lake Jackson with the roads from Pleasant Hill to Interstate 10 iced over. The one nice apartment complex in Lake Jackson was full, mainly of teachers. I was able to get a room in the home of one of our older math teachers. I found out pretty quickly that she was a local legend and that you did what Allie Lovett wanted you to do.

I soon became friends with several young teachers. Some are friends to this day. After school, I would run home, change clothes and go to the apartments before Allie got home. I spent most of my time there in the evenings. I do not know when I prepared my lessons. I missed James terribly, and my trips to the apartment in the evening were a relief. He made several trips to Lake Jackson. This was very hard on him, especially with the heavy burden of those senior engineering courses. A fellow teacher, Merry Brown, convinced me that I should spend the summer with her and another teacher in New Mexico. She had jobs lined up for us as counselors in a Girl Scout camp in the mountains above Santa Fe. I weighed the opportunity carefully, talked it over with James, and decided that it might be a good idea. If I went home for the summer, I knew it would be a distraction for him. He was graduating in August and did not need me around. He had already accepted a job with Monsanto in Luling, Louisiana, near New Orleans. A mishap on one of those last engineering courses would not have been good. I went to New Mexico. What an experience it turned out to be! There is no way that I will get started on this one. It would take another book and much of it would be censored.

By the time I returned from New Mexico, Daddy had accepted a job in Baton Rouge as director of School Food Services and Commodity Distribution. This department had one of the largest budgets in the State of Louisiana. James graduated in August and set out for Luling, Louisiana, where the Monsanto plant was located and also where we were to live. I got home late in August. Daddy, who was already in his office at the state capitol, had called Superintendent Dick Vial in St. Charles parish, arranging for a job for me. I was hired for a teaching position in seventh grade science at Luling Elementary School, incidentally, without my knowledge or an interview. Daddy was still taking care of me. By the end of August, Mother had arrived in Baton Rouge and James and I were settled in Luling, about an hour from Baton Rouge. By the way, Daddy helped Mother get a position at an elementary school in an upscale area of the city. Mother worked as hard there as she did in Pleasant Hill, this time without the stress. Over the years, mother became friends with some great ladies in Baton Rouge. They went to social events, plays, lunch, and did all kinds of things that mother was unable to do before. In a way, I suppose she found a wider world also. The parents of her students were among some of the most affluent people in Baton Rouge and they seemed to appreciate her intelligence and teaching skills. I might add that she eventually became a media specialist and librarian at her school. When the principal, Mona Terry, was off campus, Mother was the acting principal.

James and I had separate apartments in Luling, but we spent every hour that we could together. Along with a gang of teachers, we would often go into New Orleans, fourteen miles from Luling, stay out all night, come home, shower and go to work. We were having the time of our lives, looking forward to November twenty-seventh, our wedding date. With Daddy's new position, we were wined and dined. My principal, Mrs. Schmidt, was a grand lady. From an old West Bank family, she actually lived out in Jefferson Parish. She gave a party for the teachers at least once a month in her home. We danced, ate freshly shucked oysters, raw and fried, and had the most wonderful time. Mr. Schmidt loved to dance with the young teachers. If he got a bit too close, Mrs. Schmidt would walk by, shake her finger in his face and say: "Charlie, remember, the pinking shears." One day, I simply could not stand it any longer so I asked her why she said that. Her reply was: "I've always told Charlie if he messed around that I would cut it off with pinking shears."

10

Newlyweds

Mrs. Schmidt gave us the most beautiful dinner party before our wedding. Mother and Daddy drove down from Baton Rouge. I will always remember Mrs. Schmidt's elegance and grace. After James and I moved to Lake Jackson, we went back to see her. At that time, she went into a closet and pulled out a large vase filled with dried flowers. She wanted me to have it, so I took it home. As my interest in antiques grew, I became more puzzled about the vase. It turned out to be a valuable piece of Loetz art glass. Loetz designed for Tiffany until he went back to Austria. It is one of my treasures.

Mother and I were consumed with getting ready for November twenty-seventh. My dress was being made in New York, and we were on pins and needles about it getting to Baton Rouge on time. The bridal consultant from Goudchaux's in Baton Rouge did our wedding. Lee was a former Miss Baton Rouge and was wonderful to us. We were getting married in the Baptist Church in Pleasant Hill, a three-hour drive from Baton Rouge, and four hours from Luling. This definitely complicated things. The dress arrived on time, and we were ready for the big day. All was well until the day of the rehearsal. James was flying to Shreveport from New Orleans and got bumped off the plane in Alexandria. I was frantic and still do not know how he made it in time. A storm came the night of our wedding. We drove to Shreveport in the storm where we spent our wedding night in the bridal suite of the Holiday Inn. Guess we

were still looking for that big, wide world! The next morning, we drove to Hot Springs for three days. We were about the only ones in Hot Springs since betting on the horses had stopped. Obviously, we did not care. We had little time since we were both working. We returned to Luling to start our lives together.

Soon after settling into our tiny, sixty-dollar-a-month apartment, I got the bright idea that I should do a science fair for Luling Elementary. The days were full of regular activities, so we worked with the kids in the evening. The "we" included James. We spent the first few weeks of our married life at school. The science fair turned out well and the new science teacher made the local paper.

Mr. and Mrs. James Kyle

Don't trip!

Daddy was a bit perturbed when we told him that we had bought a twenty-four foot aluminum hull cabin cruiser. No house, no money, but we had a big blue boat. In the two years that we were in Luling, we explored the swamps and bayous around the area. With the help of our Cajun landlord, we drove the boat all the way from Des Allemands through Lake Salvador to Lafitte to see the pirogue races. Lake Salvador was full of sting rays during those years. We lost many hooks to the rays.

Living in South Louisiana was the continuation of my expanded world. It was there than I experienced a new culture and a new breed of folks. Soon, we moved from the tiny apartment to a nice, larger house. Our parents, as well as other relatives, could visit us. Daddy loved the big, blue boat. He would sit on the front and take everything in. We learned a lot about those swamps. They can be deadly, yet so beautiful. We purchased topographical maps of Bayou Gauche and other nearby areas. With our maps and each other, we navigated some pretty scary paths. I suppose we were fearless in those days. I cannot imagine how time after time, we launched that big, heavy boat. Shortly after purchasing it, we replaced two older thirty-five horse power motors with a new hundred ten horse power Mercury. At that time, it was probably the largest outboard motor that Mercury made.

A happy two-some

I vividly remember one of those times when we were pulling the boat out of the bayou. My job was to keep the boat straight so that it would ride up the trailer properly. Naturally, I had to stand in the water. Things did not go well that day, so I was in the water quite a while. Suddenly, I felt this stinging around the top of my socks. I ran to the bank, took off my socks only to find a band of small leeches attached to my skin around the top of my socks. We pulled them off one by one. I learned a valuable lesson that day. Never wade in a South Louisiana bayou without waders.

After Hurricane Betsy, James and I were exploring a bayou in the vicinity of Lake Des Allemands. The banks of the bayous in South Louisiana are, for the most part, marsh. As we motored along, I noticed an old, hand-carved pirogue sitting on top of the marsh. I was determined to take this little artifact home. It almost cost me my life. I told James to motor up to the edge of the marsh. I jumped out of the boat into the sloppy mud in an attempt to retrieve the pirogue. I tied a rope to it and began to pull it toward the boat. A few feet from the water, I felt myself sinking into the mud. At this point, I could not move. I'm still holding tight to the pirogue rope. We were in a small skiff that we had purchased from a friend. Thank goodness, we were not in "ole blue." James put the bow of the boat into the marsh where I could reach it. As he put the motor in reverse, I held on to the boat for dear life. He literally pulled me out of the mud with the skiff. In a few years, that pirogue actually made its way to Lake Jackson, Texas.

11

Life in Luling

Mr. and Mrs. Schmidt loved us and we loved them. I believe we became the kids they never had. Mr. Schmidt was a member of the Krewe of Okeanos, one of the best Mardi Gras krewes. After we got married, Mr. Schmidt started working on getting James into the Krewe. Eventually he did. You have never been to a party until you have been to a Krewe of Okeanos party! We went to the Krewe ball even before James became a member. The big Mardi Gras balls in New Orleans are indescribable. It was disappointing to us that we left for Pascagoula before James was able to ride the floats.

Frequently, Daddy traveled back and forth to Washington for National meetings at the Department of Agriculture. Orville Freeman was Secretary of Agriculture during this time, and he and Daddy became friends. At these meetings, Daddy met other State directors. Two women, one the Director in Maryland, and the other in Georgia, hit Daddy up for an invitation to a Mardi Gras Ball. His secretary, Gerry White, was a member of the La. Pen Women, a distinguished group of writers. She never made a mistake in her letters or the speeches she edited for Daddy. Mrs. Schmidt got the invitations and plans were made for the two ladies to come to New Orleans to the Krewe of Okeanos ball. Gerry was handling everything. Daddy told Gerry to send them a note saying James would pick them up at the airport and that they could easily recognize him because he would be wearing a red ribbon in his pocket and was six feet, four inches tall and weighed two hundred pounds. Gerry typed four feet, six inches instead of what Daddy had written. She got the two hundred pounds right. After we got to know the two women, they confessed that when they got the letters, they were horrified. They could not imagine walking around New Orleans with a four foot, six inch, two hundred pound freak. When they saw James with his red ribbon, they breathed a sigh of relief. They loved the ball, the plantation tours and especially the food. The chef at the Commander's Palace in New Orleans did cooking demonstrations for Daddy at his state meetings for Parish Supervisors of School Lunch. We had dinner there one night and the chef cooked our meal tableside. The ladies were thrilled.

Living in Luling was like living in New Orleans without the problems of the city, only fourteen miles away. In spite of its reputation, New Orleans is still a wonderful city with so many great things to do. We loved Pete Fountain and Al Hirt. They both had clubs in the French Quarter when we lived in New Orleans. We went to hear them many times. Sometimes, we would even drop by Pat O'Brien's Club for a hurricane. Even with my Southern Baptist background, I have been known to take a nip or two. Living in South Louisiana did not help much. The first year I was at Luling Elementary, Dick Vial, the superintendent, gave a barbecue for the new teachers at what he called his palmetto ranch. I started through the line and made my way toward the drink barrels. I ordered a coke. The guy serving the drinks said, "Sorry, Cher. All we have is Pearl, Jax and Schlitz." For me, that was an eye-opening experience. I had become part of a fascinating culture.

Shortly after we moved into our little apartment, I decided that I should make James a lemon pie. I located my Better Homes and Gardens Cookbook. It was a wedding present. I found a lemon pie recipe which called for one-fourth cup of fresh lemon juice. I did not have fresh lemons, so I looked in the pantry and found a bottle of lemon extract. I thought at the time that it would be okay to substitute the extract for the fresh lemon juice, so I put one fourth cup of lemon extract in the pie. I have no earthly idea why I had lemon extract. I could not wait for James to get home from work. I greeted him at the door with "I baked you a lemon pie." After we ate, I cut him a piece of pie. When he bit into it, his lips turned wrong side out. How he ate that pie, I will never know. "Honey, your pie was better than my mama's pie," were his only words.

I cannot leave Luling without this story. Here, we rode out hurricane Betsy. This is the year that we were in the tiny apartment. One of my teacher friends invited us to stay with them. Betsy hit us during the night with a vengeance. We thought that we would go every minute. As the eye passed over, we decided to get in bed before the winds started again. If we were not going to make it, at least, we would be together. It is hard to believe that we went off to sleep. When we woke at daylight, the winds had subsided. We looked out the window to see the house across the street leveled. We were frightened for the family. They were saved because they got into their car, which was in the garage. The garage was the only thing left standing. Our little apartment had minor damage. I will remember that horrible night all the days of my life.

One of my biggest concerns the next morning was the school. James and I made our way to Luling Elementary through tons of debris. When we arrived, we found my classroom filled with a foot of purple water mixed with rock and tar from the caved in ceiling. One wall of the school was pushed in several inches. Back in those days, we used purple carbons to run off tests and activity sheets. I had a stack of those in my bottom desk drawer. They floated out as the water came up. The water came from rain, not from rising water. What a purple mess this was! The kids who did not have damage to their homes walked to school and helped shovel wheel barrow loads of mess from the classrooms. Would kids today do that? I hope so.

12

Pascagoula

Although the years at Luling were wonderful, James was becoming increasingly unhappy at Monsanto. We talked it over and he accepted a job with a private consulting firm in New Orleans. We were excited because we expected to stay in Luling with the new job. Right before school was out that year, the company asked him to take a consulting job at Standard Oil of Kentucky in Pascagoula, Mississippi. In addition to his salary, we would receive five hundred fifty dollar *per diem* each month. This was more than I was making. In 1966, that was big money. I said, "Let's go." We rented a lovely two story brick home overlooking the Gulf in Gautier for three hundred a month. Gautier was across the river from Pascagoula. The subdivision had a canal that led into the Gulf. This was great for our big blue boat. We tied her to the bulkhead on the side of the canal. After work, weather permitting, we took her out to the oyster reef which was only three-hundred yards from shore. We loaded up on flounder and sand trout every day that we fished. We threw hundreds of sand trout back because they do not freeze well. They are good eating when cooked fresh. On weekends, we would venture out to Horn Island with its beautiful sand beach. The water there was clear and beautiful, probably because it was fourteen or so miles off shore. We swam, picnicked, and, of course, fished.

Eventually, we made the decision to keep "ole blue" at a nearby marina. It became obvious that she was getting slower and slower. James spoke to the marina owner about it. He suggested that we pull her out of the water and take a look. We did and found that the entire bottom was covered with barnacles. Our barnacle scraping parties became well known. We learned about anti-fouling paint the hard way.

As summer began to fade, I decided that I had better look for a job. I first went to the Pascagoula School Board Office. They seemed interested in my qualifications; however, I had not taken the National Teacher Exam which they required. I then went three miles up the River to Moss Point. The first question that I was asked was, "What can you teach?" I muttered, "English and science." The second question followed. "Can you teach math?" I said yes without a great deal of confidence. The Moss Point Schools hired me on the spot to teach seventh grade math and science.

James and I agree that this year in Pascagoula was one of our best. I was assigned to Carl Eley Elementary School, and greeted warmly by the older than usual faculty. They seemed happy to see a young twenty-three year old appear. They took me under their wings and I loved it. Moss Point is a beautiful town scattered with a fair number of old southern mansions. I soon found out that one of the teachers lived in one. Soon after school started, Louise sent us an invitation to a party at her "Mansion". When we drove up to the old southern home that evening, we were mesmerized by the white columns and manicured yard. At the door, we were greeted warmly by a black butler. I'm thinking that I must be getting closer and closer to that wider world. Upon entering, we saw southern elegance at its finest. Black waiters were passing around trays of hors d'oeuvres and drinks. At dinner, the main course was quail. Halfway through dinner, James whispered that he felt sick because the quail was not agreeing with him. Since so many people were at the long table, I decided that it would not be noticed if he got up. I whispered back to him that he should excuse himself and go outside for some fresh air. I was finally able to leave the table to see about him. As I made my way through the large yard, I found him sitting on a bench, sick as a dog. It was not the quail. It was the Jack Daniels. Needless to say, he was in bad trouble with his wife.

The school year turned out to be one of a kind. I took the kids out in the yard for little demonstrations and show and tells. Often, other seventh grade teachers would bring their kids out to watch. I remember that I did a volcano eruption using ammonium dichromate. This chemical, when ignited, presents the most realistic volcano eruption possible. This is a highly toxic chemical; however, I had the presence of mind to do it outside and keep the kids far away. In later years, I would have been in big trouble for doing this. The kids loved it, and begged me to do it over and over. The principal let me do pretty much what I wanted. After working under Mrs. Schmidt, this was something. From time to time, I would walk my kids down to the Pascagoula River when the tide was out. We crawled down into the empty tidal zone and dug in the banks for fossils and small animals. One day, one of the students found a perfect point, probably from the Pascagoula Tribe. I have it to this day.

At work, James got friend

Aunt Gladys and Aunt Edna

ly with another engineer from the firm. He and his wife became great friends. Both were Cajuns from the heart of bayou country. We formed a little band with Bob and James on the guitar, me on the piano, and Opal on the drums. We played in our garage many evenings with the entire neighborhood swinging and swaying. We were never very good, but we had a great time. I can still hear Opal belting out "Poison Ivy". Also, Opal and Bob learned how to scrape barnacles.

One of the kids in my two-hour math and science class at Carl Eley was named Noel Lamey. I can see his little seventh grade face as I write this. He was one of the sweetest kids that I ever taught. I was in love with the name Noel and vowed that if I ever had a son, I would name him Noel and we did.

There have been so many special people in my life over the years. None were more special than Daddy's sister, Aunt Edna and Mother's sister, Aunt Gladys. Aunt Edna's only daughter was killed in a bicycle accident when she was ten years old. Her husband died soon after. Aunt Gladys and Uncle Tommy Farr had two boys who were raised like brothers to me. To this day, I love them dearly. The older son, Al, is five years my junior. John is ten years younger than I am.

Since I was not working that first summer in Pascagoula, we invited everybody to come. Aunt Gladys and John flew from Shreveport on an old prop plane. I can still picture John coming out of that plane with his fishing rods dangling all over the place. Every day, we would strike out to the back bays to fish. One day, Aunt Gladys hooked something that she fought for ages. She never did land it. It finally broke her line. We concluded that it was a submerged flying saucer. This was about the time that people were seeing "unidentified flying objects" all over the place.

My "brothers" Al and John

Soon after, Al showed up with two of his buddies, both of whom were just finishing high school. Al had grown up with these boys, so James and I knew them well. Al, Craig, and Raymond were three peas in a pod. Al called and said not to worry, they were bringing food. They showed up with a six pack of beer and a package of Oreo Cookies. We had a party almost every night. They spent a good deal of time chasing the curvaceous daughter of our friends from Biloxi. On one of those nights, Al got a bit looped. His Mother called. I panicked, and so did he. You have never in your life seen anybody sober up so fast. The boys could not wait until James got home from work so that we could go out in the boat. One afternoon, we were raking in the fish. All of a sudden, a big coast guard cutter came up beside us, right in the spot where we were fishing. They asked if we needed help. James replied, "No." The coast guard officer said, "Well, someone was waving a white flag from the top of the boat." It turned out that Raymond was on top of the boat, waving his shirt in the air to dry it. We were ready to kill him.

13

The West Bank

Toward the end of the school year, James was told that he was being transferred back to the home office in New Orleans. I stayed in Pascagoula to finish the year while James reported to work in New Orleans. He stayed in the Firm apartment above the office on Baronne Street. One morning, he came down to find his 1956 Chevy totally stripped. That car was so much a part of us. We had fogged up the windows in it at Louisiana Tech, and I had driven it to practice teach at the Tech lab school for an entire semester.

We settled into a rent house in Gretna, across the River from New Orleans. At the same time, we purchased a black Volkswagen for James to drive to work. I continued to drive the 1963 Super Sports Chevrolet that Daddy and Mother had given me for college graduation. Leaving Pascagoula was sad for us. Once again, I stepped into a teaching position. I was assigned to teach science at Westwego Junior High, truly a blackboard jungle school. It was several miles up the West Bank Expressway to the school. A chain link fence surrounded the school. The fence kept the kids in and the trouble makers out. This speaks to the environment in which I worked. I also helped coach the girls' basketball team. James would drive to the school on game nights to see me safely home. One night, my car was vandalized. We had to have the locks changed. My desk in the classroom was broken into and my lunch money stolen. I had a kid come at me with a coke bottle because he was unhappy that I had not allowed him to enter a certain door. Thankfully, he had second thoughts.

The only place that we could park our boat was in the front yard. One night someone came into the yard, unbolted the hundred ten horse power Mercury and took off with it. Experience taught us what a tough place New Orleans can be.

14

Returning to Lake Jackson

James was very happy with private consulting. He was paid well and liked his bosses. In spite of this, he put his name in with a headhunter, mostly as a fishing expedition. He started getting calls from all over the country. We realized more and more how bad things were where we lived. With an expensive motor stolen and a car stripped, we began to rethink our life. One of the calls that he continued to get was from a recruiter who represented a company partly owned by Dow Chemical in Freeport, Texas. We flew to Houston and drove down to Freeport for an interview. It was my first plane ride, and I was scared to death. Flying has never been my bag although I have flown many times. James was offered a job. We returned home and began to deliberate. The big issue was whether or not I could return to Brazosport Independent School District. James continued to say, "Becky, I hope that we will have children one day and we do not want to raise them here." I picked up the telephone and called Lake Jackson Junior High. At that time, Mr. Grady Rasco was still principal. When I left Lake Jackson to get married, Mr. Rasco had said to me, "Miss Stoker, if you will work at it, I think you will be a pretty good teacher one day." Mavis, Mr. Rasco's secretary, answered the phone, and I explained my situation. Mr. Rasco hired me to teach physical science. The rest is history.

We moved to Lake Jackson in the summer of 1968. Mother and Daddy helped us buy the house that we live in today. It was on a large lot and over the years, we have added a covered pool, guest house and a four hundred square foot workshop. We have never wanted to leave our neighborhood and several of the original neighbors remain today. James likes to tell that he floored the attic in July of 1968. This South Texas heat made him remember that for years.

In those early years, we made life-long friends. Linda Holt taught science right across the hall. She and her husband Ben became fast friends. One cold winter day, James, Ben, and I went duck hunting in the Brazos River Swamp. Yes, there are swamps in Texas, too. Ben shot a wood duck, and it fell into the slough. James said, "Ben, you will have to let the duck go because it's too cold to go get it. Ben replied, "James, that's a good duck. That's a good duck and I'm going to get it." Ben had a habit of repeating himself. He told me to walk up the road around the curve. He stripped off naked and went into the water to get the duck. Much to my horror, as I rounded the curve, I saw a truck coming down that wet, muddy road. I began calculating my strategy because I knew that those people would not take kindly to a naked Ben coming out of the slough with a dead duck. I marked time by flagging the folks down and explaining that the road ahead was very slippery. The people in the truck, including a woman, probably wondered why I wanted to stand in the middle of a muddy road on a cold winter day and chat. Thankfully, Ben got his clothes on before they passed.

Joyce Stafford was one of our physical education teachers. We were friends during my earlier one-semester stay at Lake Jackson Junior High. By the time I returned, Mr. Rasco had been promoted to Assistant Superintendent and a great guy named Jim Cashion was made principal. During my three-and-a-half year absence, Joyce got married to Chuck Barefield. They became our best friends. We did everything together, including fishing, walking the railroads for date nails, going out dancing and traveling together. Because they were such an integral part of our lives for many years, they will be mentioned many times in this book. Although, Chuck has passed away, Joyce, James, and I are still very close.

Teaching physical science was tough for me. Thankfully, James walked me through the hard parts. I was basically a biology and English teacher. Later on, I went back to the University of Houston and acquired fifty-five hours of pure science above my bachelor's degree. Chris Crainer taught science across the hall from me for years. Chris was such fun! We protected each other and shared our problems for years. Chris and I decided to work on our Master's together. For one summer, one night a week, after school, we would drive to the University of Houston campus in Clear Lake. The fog could be so bad coming home that Chris would hang out the window to see if I was still on the road.

The last class that we took was educational psychology. The professor was boring and read her entire lecture. Chris and I would get tickled and could not stop laughing. We got called down twice. Soon, I told Chris that we must separate or get thrown out of a graduate level class. She agreed and moved. Unfortunately, I could still see her out of the corner of my eye. This particular night, part of the lecture was about the psychologist, Fred Rogers. Chris is very smart; however, I instinctively, knew that she did not know who Fred Rogers was. I saw her hand go up and under my breath began to mutter, "No, Chris, no!" Out it came. Chris asked: "Is that the Mr. Rogers on TV?" At least one hundred graduate students found it funny. The professor was not amused. She was still trying to figure out why two idiots were in her graduate level class. On the way home that foggy evening, Chris pulled her head back in the car to say, "Becky, let's quit." I answered, "Okay. Let's do." That ended our Master's pursuit. After all, we both had young children. It didn't matter. We ended up making as much money because of the newly-instituted career ladder.

Chris and Everett Crainer also became good couple friends. One weekend, we all went out to Bandera to our deer lease. That was a special weekend! Everett climbed up one of the mountains to hunt with a bottle of Boone's Farm Wine. He went to sleep and did not show up back in camp. We were frantic. Chris was not too happy when he stumbled into camp. James wanted me to kill a doe for sausage, so Chris and I set off to the blind together. We climbed up into the blind and settled down, waiting for a doe to appear. Chris kept saying: "If that doe doesn't show up, I'm going to pee in my pants." I told her to be quiet, or we would never see a doe. In due time, a big doe appeared. I was having trouble getting her in my sights. Chris was getting more agitated. Finally, I dropped the doe. Chris pushed me out of my chair and jumped the seven feet to the ground. Chris and I never hunted together again.

15

Teaching in Lake Jackson

I loved teaching in Lake Jackson. Our parents were caring and educated and appreciated our efforts. Our students came from homes where education was valued and encouraged. I am sorry to say that our demographics have changed in recent years. With my broad-field science certification, I felt comfortable in whatever I was asked to teach. Many of those left over sections fell to me, although life science or biology was my real love. In later years, I wrote the curriculum and taught the life science search or gifted program. My dear friend, Jean Sanders, was in charge of this program. I knew Jean from earlier years when I taught her son Scott. Scott became a very successful architect.

I decided to include an anatomy unit in my search curriculum. We normally dissected small animals in life science. The dogfish shark was a new ballgame. The kids loved it. The dogfish that I purchased from Carolina Biological were viviparous. As we got further into the dogfish, I heard one of the girl's scream. "It's got babies." The other kids rushed over to watch her remove the baby dogfish. Gifted kids are not always neat or orderly. Even with me barking all of the time, they would inevitably throw the guts in the lab sinks. One day, I was really tired from breathing formaldehyde and running from lab station to lab station. I have a chronic lung problem to this day from breathing formaldehyde for all of those years. As I moved around the room, I saw that the sinks were full of dissected parts. Half of them were stopped up. I shouted at the top of my lungs: "Get that crap out of those sinks!" After that, the sinks stayed clean. Over time, my beloved Granny Stoker added a few choice words to my vocabulary. Thank God, I said "crap" instead of one of those golden oldies.

When I reflect over my work years, I have no regrets about my decision to enter and remain in education. I had opportunities over the years to leave teaching; yet, a powerful magnet always pulled me back. I expect that this magnet has to do with my love for children. I have fought publicly and privately for improved benefits for teachers, retirement benefits in particular. One of my primary goals was to encourage teachers to participate in their communities and get involved in the political arena. I am proud that teachers have now realized the power of political involvement. Our local and state teacher organizations are a powerful force in Austin these days.

There are so many stories relating to my thirty-eight years in the classroom that could be told. It is hard to know which ones should be told. After Mr. Cashion was made an assistant principal at Brazoswood High School, we inherited a new administration at Lake Jackson Intermediate School. Sandra Lea was librarian and a close friend. My lab was at the end of a long hall. A door opened into a small storage room which led to the library. This small room was the place where Sandra and I met to vent or to discuss important secrets. It was the last period of the day. The principal came on the loud speaker. "Will all minority students come to the cafeteria?" My kids began raising their hands and asking me if they were a minority. I was distressed that my students were being singled out this way. A few students went to the cafeteria, most remained. I dismissed class and told the kids that they could visit. Off I went to the "private room." Sandra was already there. "Did I hear that right?" Sandra answered. "Yes, and we are going to have some trouble over this one." I agreed. Things rocked on. Sandra and I concluded that we had escaped any problems. Unexpectedly, several weeks later, up shows Channel 13, the ABC affiliate in Houston. A parent had reported the incident. We made the news!

John Faseler was one of our assistant principals under this new administration. He was a great guy and the teachers loved him. We had a close relationship over the years, and I was happy that I was able to teach his boys. John told me later that this was not a computer decision. I am still flattered. At this point, I was in charge of the science stockroom. I usually worked there during my conference period. Some days, John would slip away to visit and escape from the daily rigors of being an assistant principal. We talked about life, school and our families. John's beautiful wife, Barbara, is a good friend. I enjoy visiting with her as much as I enjoyed my visits with John. John passed away after a valiant fight with ALS, commonly known as Lou Gehrig's Disease. Everyone who knew John was devastated.

Mr. Cashion asked me to take over the stockroom job shortly after he became principal. I agreed reluctantly. It did pay a nice stipend, so this helped my decision. Since no one had been in charge of the stockroom, it was in terrible shape. One of my pet peeves was that teachers were allowed to smoke in it with all of the flammable chemicals. The first thing I did, with Mr. Cashion's permission, was to put up No Smoking signs. The second thing was to get a chemist from Dow out to help me go through the chemicals. When he saw the chemical shelves, he roped off the hall and took most of the chemicals to be destroyed. The No Smoking signs annoyed the smokers, and they gave me a hard time. Then, I was carrying around a few extra pounds. One day, one of the disgruntled smokers told me, "Becky, you fuss at us all the time about smoking, but you're overweight and that's just as bad." As I got older, I didn't take much guff off of anybody. I replied, "That's true, but I don't go around blowing my fat in your face." I never heard another word about smoking in the science stockroom.

16

Our Travels Begin

Sometime after we moved to Lake Jackson, James was sent to California to computer school at what is now known as Silicon Valley. It was in the summer, and I was able to go with him. It became the honeymoon we never had. That wider world was continuing to open up for me. I ate my first fresh salmon at a waterside restaurant in Sausalito. It was good, but not as good as the grilled salmon that James fixes today. One afternoon, we took the harrowing trip up Mount Hamilton to Lick Observatory. As we drove up, it appeared that they were closing. I approached one of the researchers and blurted out that I was a science teacher from Texas and wanted so badly to see the observatory. He surprised me with "I'll just open back up for you." We got a private tour. I was given tons of pictures taken through the telescope which was at that time one of the biggest in the world. I gave them to an Earth Science teacher at school, and I guess they got tossed. Sadly, light pollution from areas below such as San Jose and Silicon Valley has become a problem. Gratefully, the University of California continues to fund Lick and researchers from all of its campuses work there.

Sometime prior to our trip, I had read that Stanford Nobel laurates hung out in a certain restaurant in Palo Alto. I was particularly familiar with Dr. Joshua Lederberg because of his work in microbial genetics. His work had been mentioned on occasion in my college classes. Dr. Lederberg shared the Nobel Prize in Medicine in 1955 with Edward Tatum and George Beadle. He found that bacteria transfer genetic information. I knew what he looked like because I had seen pictures of him in my college textbooks. As I write this, I cannot remember the name of the restaurant; however, we went there for dinner one evening. We were seated and given our menu. I looked across at an adjacent table and there sat Dr. Joshua Lederberg with a group of probable Nobel laurates. I could not get up enough courage to speak to him. I figured that he was not interested in wasting his time with a young teacher from Pleasant Hill. At the very least, I can brag about having dinner with a Nobel Prize winner.

I remember how willing James was to take me different places on that trip. He has always treated me with love and kindness. Mostly, he lets me have my way. I am sure there are times that he would love to bite my head off. I can be intense, and he is Mr. Easy Going. Mother told me once that people said that our marriage would not last a year. I guess they figured that the only child syndrome would get us. They were wrong! It has been a fifty-three year love affair. I might add that I am one of the few people who can make James really angry. Oh well, include the kids in that.

The time sequence of our early years in Lake Jackson is often unclear to me. After we got the kids, things seemed to come together better. In the early 1980's, James and I took a trip to New York City. He secured reservations at the Waldorf and tickets to two of the biggest shows on Broadway. We flew from Houston to New York. As we were making our final approach, I noticed that we were beginning to climb again. I have earlier noted my dislike of flying. In a panic, I told James that we were climbing and of course, he said that I was being silly. The pilot came on the intercom with this little gem: "Ladies and gentlemen, we're going to give you a tour of Manhattan while we check into a little problem." The co-pilot then walked down the aisle to the rear of the plane. On the way back, James stopped him and asked what was going on. He told us that they had a light showing that the landing gear was not locked. He had walked to the back of the plane to visually check. Finally, we made the final approach again at which time, we landed safely. The runway was lined with ambulances, fire trucks and foam trucks. I was so scared that I remembered a few of my granny's words.

We arrived at the Waldorf eager to explore this great city. After checking in, we went to our room, deposited our luggage and took off to see the sights. We returned to the hotel to get ready for our first Broadway play. It happened to be the Tony-winning play, *Woman of the Year* with Lauren Bacall and Harry Guardino. I recall that Lauren Bacall got tickled about something and forgot her lines. We had reservations at Sardi's after the play. I told James that he should not allow us to get saddled with a bad table. We arrived at the restaurant, at which time, James offered the maître d' a big ten dollars to give us a good table. The maître d' refused the ten dollars with the comment: "Don't worry, Sir. I'll give you a good table." (James has always been frugal when it comes to tipping.) After we were seated, I said, "James, you just tried to tip Vincent Sardi ten dollars." We did get an excellent table. I recognized Vincent Sardi because he was doing Heinz Catsup commercials on TV at the time.

We ordered, enjoyed our meal and prepared to receive our check. I looked up to see Elizabeth Taylor walk in. Rock Hudson was right behind her. She was appearing in *Little Foxes* on Broadway. We had tried to get tickets to see her; however, the play was sold out for weeks. I told James that we could not possibly leave now. As the waiter brought our check, he said, "We'll never get out of here. She stays half the night and Mr. Sardi will not close when she is here." It is amazing to me how many details I am remembering from years ago, especially since I can't remember what happened five minutes ago. The bar at Sardi's was separated from the restaurant by white lattice. We retreated to the bar where we watched Elizabeth Taylor by peeping through the lattice. I have never seen a diamond as big as the one Elizabeth Taylor was wearing, compliments of Richard Burton. The only others in the bar were a businessman and a pretty young thing. As we peeped through the lattice together, I suspicioned that she was not his wife. We finally got tired of peeping and went back to the hotel.

When we entered our room, it appeared that someone had been there and messed up the bed. I convinced James that someone had been in our room. He promptly called down to the desk and reported our intruder. As he hung up the phone, a funny look came over his face. "What did they say?", I asked. With a big grin on his face, he reported, "They said, "Sir, you are at the Waldorf Astoria and we turn back your covers and place a chocolate on your pillow." In our defense, whoever did our covers must have been in a big hurry. The next day, we went to the Rainbow Room for lunch. It was a surprise to run into the businessman and pretty young thing there. Our last night in New York, we saw *Sugar Babies* with Mickey Rooney and Ann Miller, who came from a little Texas town called Chireno, near Nacogdoches.

Joyce, Chuck, James and I bought some property near Pagosa Springs, Colorado, sight unseen. After a year or two, we decided to go check it out. Mother and Daddy had gotten to know Chuck and Joyce, so they wanted to go. The six of us took off to Colorado. We walked railroad tracks from Texas to Colorado, looking for date nails. We collected hundreds. I do not recall that we had reservations anywhere on the trip. We just rode and found a place. One evening, we found a beautiful spot. We could look up and see Mesa Verde in the distance. The cabins were owned by an old couple and their unmarried daughter. The amenities included small cabins and stocked trout ponds. Daddy and Chuck immediately began fishing. When Daddy found out that he was paying by the pound, trout began to find their way back into the water.

The old couple told us a great story. A year or two before, a big buck deer came up to their house every evening. They fed the deer and it became a pet. With hunting season approaching, they became afraid that it would be shot. A red sweater was placed on the deer. It was a great relief when hunting season was over. "Big Buck" appeared one day with the sweater still on.

The funniest part of this story involves a bottle of Jack Daniels that Chuck and James had bought the day before. James told Chuck to get the bottle out of the car and take it into his room before Daddy could see it. Chuck, sitting in the back seat of the suburban, was able to accomplish the task. He put the bottle in a drawer in his room. Daddy always rode in the front. Daddy stepped from the car and began exploring everything, including everyone's rooms. Soon thereafter, he appeared with the bottle of Jack. He said, "Look what somebody left in the room." My Baptist deacon daddy promptly tossed the unopened bottle into a garbage can.

Carolyn and Larry Parks are good friends of ours. Carolyn is a precious, kind, Christian lady. I love her dearly! Larry has written a two-volume book on fishing. It has been well received. One chapter is about fishing with James. Larry also writes a column for our local paper. Recently he devoted a column to James. Larry and James have caught some beautiful redfish. On one trip, James caught a whopper of a flounder. He stuffed it with shrimp and crabmeat. Not only was it delicious, it was beautiful when he took it from the oven. Hopefully, these great fishing days will continue.

In later years, James traveled extensively. For the most part, he went to South America, Europe and Canada. He made my friends and fellow teachers happy by bringing semi-precious stones from Brazil to them over the years. He brought amethyst, citrine quartz, opals, blue topaz and emeralds from Colombia for Amy and me. I was especially happy with the emeralds he bought for me in Colombia. Mother was always on his gift list. A confession finally came that he had a bodyguard when he was in Colombia. The bodyguard was an ex-Columbian marine who was tough as nails and carried a 45 under his belt. He called James "Big Jim". When James returned home, he bought baseballs, a glove and other items for the guy's son. I guess he sent the stuff in the Dow mail because it got there. The bodyguard was thrilled with the gifts. By the time he retired, James had logged over eight hundred thousand air miles.

17

Our Children

After eleven years of marriage and plenty of trying, it became clear that we would probably not be able to have biological children. After many tears and late night discussions, we started the adoption process. We applied to the Methodist Mission Home in San Antonio and Saint Mark's in Houston. Our application was accepted by both. After much heartfelt discussion, we decided to use the Methodist Home. At that time, we had no idea what adopting a child involved. I will always believe that my dear friend and mentor, Georgia Walley, was responsible for our success with the Methodist Mission Home. She made arrangements for us to meet with Dr. Perry Rankin, who was pastor of the First Methodist Church in Lake Jackson. Soon after our visit with Dr. Rankin, the wheels began to turn. The home visits began, one unannounced. Our financial records were scrutinized, our closets were checked, and our references contacted. Our final hurdle was the interview with the director of the home.

We left for the interview in San Antonio early in the morning, arriving shortly after noon. I was a nervous wreck. James was his usual calm self. We were greeted warmly and the interview began. The first question to James was: "Tell me three reasons why you love your wife." Without a blink, he came forth with three great answers. The next question was for me: "Tell me three reasons why you love your husband." My mind went completely blank. I knew that I loved James more than anything on this Earth. I just could not remember why! A long pause ensued and out came: "I love the way he loves me." That was the only thing I could think of. The soul-searching interview continued. It was very personal and emotional. I guess I did okay on the other questions. On the way home, James said, "Becky, I love the way you love me, too, but why couldn't you think of two more ways?"

Surprisingly, we were approved. We were told that placement would be a minimum of six months away. We went back to work thinking that we would have plenty of time to put a nursery together. The nurse's office was right next to my classroom. If I got an occasional call, I took it in Mary's office. Mary Smock was the school nurse and another of my dearest and best friends. Two weeks after the interview, Mary stuck her head in my door to tell me that I had a call. I followed her to the office and picked up the phone. A voice on the phone said, "This is the Methodist Mission Home. We have a baby girl for you and James." Mary, seeing the look on my face, slipped a chair under me to keep me from falling. Mary found Mr. Cashion. He came right down and put his arm around me. "You call Jim, go home, and take care of things. We will handle everything here." Jim Cashion was one of the finest men I have ever known.

The teachers told me later that after the call, I was walking up the hall repeating, "I haven't read the book, I haven't read the book." Dr. Spock, I'm sorry! It must be clarified that we only used "the book" for medical information. I did wear it out. During this next twenty-four hour period, James and I experienced the greatest outpouring of love that we had ever seen. The only thing we had in the nursery was a baby bed. While we were shopping at the newly-opened mall, friends were filling our house with baby clothes, diapers, food and everything else. Everyone seemed so happy that God had brought this precious baby girl into our lives. I neglected to say that we were instructed to come get Amy the next day. After twenty-four hours of no sleep, we started off to San Antonio to get our baby. It was love at first sight. After a short presentation service, we headed home with our baby girl. James still calls her baby girl and she is forty-one.

We had selected a name for a boy and one for a girl. The girl's name was Amy Lynn. As we put our four day old in her little car seat in the back of the Suburban, I smelled something. I got into the car and after a mile or so, I said, "James, I think she's pooped in her pants." He told me to crawl into the back and see. At least, I knew how to figure this one out. I related to James that indeed, she had. "Well, change her." Suddenly, it occurred to me that I had never changed a diaper in my life. I started crying. "We can change her when we get to that rest stop in Seguin." This was one of the few times that he ever screamed at me! "How would you like to have poop in your pants all the way to Seguin?" As soon as he could, he stopped, got out of the car and ordered, "You drive." He changed Amy's diaper and held her all of the way home. I suddenly remembered a second reason why I love this good man.

Later, we asked about the fast placement of Amy. We knew that many couples had been waiting a long time. Our social worker told us that the staff struggled for two days over the decision. The conclusion was that Amy was meant for our home.

As we turned into Lake Forest, Joyce and Chuck were watching from their kitchen window. James insisted that Amy was hungry and I should feed her. I poured the formula into a clean bottle, warmed it and started to feed her. By this time, Joyce and Chuck had showed up. Amy was fretful and seemed to be sucking on the bottle with difficulty. As we were trying to figure out what was going on, Joyce asked me if I had put a hole in the nipple. My reply was that I thought that it had a hole in it. We corrected the problem, and Amy became a happy camper. To this day, I can't figure out how Joyce knew that the nipple didn't have a hole in it.

A precious lady, Georgia Kendrick, came into our home to keep Amy. After Noel arrived, she kept both of them as long as she could. Eventually, Kendrick took Amy to nursery school in the mornings. This helped her manage Noel. I will be forever grateful to Georgia for the care that she gave our children.

The inclusion of the following story is the only thing in this book that James and I disagreed about. Hopefully, it will not offend anyone. I have tried to tell it in the least offensive way. When the children were small, we did not hide from them if we were undressing or showering. This was my idea because that is the way I was raised. Of course, as they got older, this changed. When Amy was about three and a half and Noel about eight months old, we decided to get a family portrait made. Prior to this event, Amy and I were reading a bedtime story. It was an animal book and she was having fun naming the parts of the animals. When she got to the horse's tail, she pointed it out and announced: "Daddy's got a tail." I about passed out. After we went to bed, I told James what had happened. He was very upset that perhaps Amy had told everyone in nursery school that her daddy had a tail. I was always the one to discuss the birds and bees. He told me that I needed to take care of this. The next day, I proceeded to explain human anatomy to my three year old, using the proper terms. It seemed to be the right thing to do at the time; however, it turned out to be a really dumb move. We forgot about the incident and planned for our family portrait. When we arrived at the hotel, the room was filled with couples waiting for engagement pictures. There was only one chair available. I sat in it while holding Noel. He was cutting a tooth and drooling all over my lap and his little shirt. James was trying to keep Amy contained. We waited for an hour. I could tell by the expressions on the faces of the prospective grooms that they had already decided not to have children. Amy was getting more and more unruly and began to grab her daddy's hands and climb up his body. Without thinking, James said, "Amy, stop, you're going to pull daddy's pants off." As loudly as she could, she said, "And daddy, your tail will pop right out." The big problem is that she did not say tail. My anatomy lesson worked! Just as this happened, we were called. Thank you, God! You have never seen two people exit a room so fast. As I ran, I noticed that the engaged couples never moved or changed expressions.

When Amy started kindergarten, I arranged for a lady to pick her up at home and deliver her to school. She was also to bring her home. This was to help Kendrick and enable her to hang on another year. The first day of school, the lady had made a doctor's appointment for her baby. She assumed that she would be out of the doctor's office in plenty of time to pick up Amy. The doctor was running late, and she got caught in an examination room. Meanwhile, Amy was the only kid waiting to be picked up. First, they called James's office. A secretary took the message and instead of finding him and giving him the message, put the message in his box. The next morning, he found the message. I have never seen him so mad. (Yes, others can make him angry.) Amy's teacher knew me, so she had the school secretary call me at school. I rushed to pick Amy up. I still laugh when I think about what the secretary said to me when she called. "Mrs. Kyle, we weren't worried. We knew that someone would pick Amy up because of that forty dollar Polly Flinder's dress." Her grandmother had bought the dress.

After both kids started school, I took them to a local day care in the mornings and picked them up there in the afternoons. I knew the owners well since I had taught their kids. They would deliver Amy and Noel to school and pick them up. The kids stayed at day care until I picked them up after school. We have always driven a Suburban and James usually had a pickup. Daddy bought his brother's old Chrysler and gave it to us. It sat in the garage for ten years after my uncle died. It still had the plastic on the seats. It was a Mack Truck and would backfire all the way around the block. I drove it to school for a year. The kids would scream and holler as we backfired our way to daycare. The old clunker still comes up in family conversations. Eventually, we decided to sell the old Chrysler. James put an ad in the paper. A woman called and wanted to test drive it. James went out to meet her and quickly returned to the house. I challenged James about letting a stranger drive off in our clunker. He retorted, "She owns a certain business on the beach, and I was not going to get in a car with her." The woman bought the car.

18

Cathy and John

Cathy and John Buettner were our next door neighbors for almost fifty years. Cathy became another of my second mothers. She did so much for us. For several years, a local dance studio did a production of "The Nutcracker." I was fundraising chair for the production. One year, on the night of dress rehearsal, Amy was running around outside while I was helping backstage. One of the dancers came inside to get me with the bad news that Amy had ripped her dress. I walked outside to find that Amy had caught her dress on a bush and ripped off ten feet of net. I rushed home with the dress and at ten o'clock in the evening, I called Cathy in tears. She consoled me. "Bring it over." After looking at the dress, Cathy said, "I'll have it fixed by tomorrow." And she did.

Cathy and John were an integral part of our lives for many years. After John passed away, Cathy stayed in the house for a while. We did our best to see about her. When she moved to a retirement home in Houston, we were brokenhearted. I miss her every day. Cathy was a true artist. What she could do with a sewing machine and a needle is well known in our town. It was Cathy who helped develop James's interest in the culinary arts. He is a wonderful cook and actually does much of the cooking. He designed a "dream kitchen" to replace our old one. At the time I thought that he was doing this for me. As the months went by, I realized he cooked more than I did.

Cathy also encouraged James to plant a garden in our back

yard. Here he grows tomatoes, beans, okra, eggplant, and cucumbers. You name it. I usually do the freezer stuff. He does the canned stuff, which includes fig preserves from his own fig tree, strawberry jam, pickled okra, pickles, and the best salsa that you have ever put your lips on. He gives away most of his canned goodies to friends and neighbors. This year, our avocado tree was prolific. We gave away tons. James is especially proud of his fruit trees. His grapefruit, blood oranges, satsumas, and lemons are pretty on the trees in the fall. We send or take boxes of fruit to North Louisiana. My cousin Skeeter thinks that James's grapefruit are the best he has ever eaten.

19

Bringing Noel Home

I was home during the summer when we got the call that we had a baby boy waiting for us. I was told that he was four months old and had undergone surgery for a condition called pyloric stenosis. I had never heard of it, so I panicked. I called James at work. He told me to call Dr. Imperial, our fantastic pediatrician. Dr. Imperial was out of the office, and Mrs. Dipple, her nurse, realizing the seriousness of the matter, put Dr. Johnson on the phone. After I explained the

Methodist Mission Home – our family

situation, he assured me that the condition was corrected by the surgery, and that one in eight newborn boys have it. His words ring in my ears to this day, "You go get that baby." Off we went to get our precious son.

Noel was a sweet child. His nature is still sweet. He loved to play with the neighborhood kids. His buddy, J.T. Lee, lived across the street and they played together for hours on end. When

Noel was in second grade, I got another bright idea. I decided that he should take piano lessons. Laura Mays, who lived in the

neighborhood, taught piano, so it seemed an easy thing to do. After a few lessons, Laura appeared at our door with Noel. She told him to go to his room and play, at which time she diplomatically said, "Becky, I think you and Jim can find a better place to put your money than piano lessons for Noel." His musical career ended right then.

Every neighborhood has a bully. The kid in ours picked on J.T. constantly. Noel was older than J.T. and very protective. One afternoon, James heard a ruckus.

Noel and J.T.

He went outside to find Noel beating the devil out of our bully.

20

Teen Years

When Amy started 10th grade, we bought her a used Toyota Corolla from my friend, Merry Brown. The first week, on the way to school, she ran into the back of a car. The mother of the girl who owned the car was a secretary at my school. Several years later, Noel demolished the front of his 300 ZX in an accident with a friend whose mother taught with me. I told the kids this: "If you kids are going to hit someone, would you please find someone who doesn't work with me." Noel and Amy called the Toyota the "crapola" car. Thank goodness, none of those kids were hurt. Noel's accident was not entirely his fault. When Amy went to college, we gave her a gold Toyota Camry coupe with Italian wheels. Noel inherited the "crapola" car. When he was a senior, we bought him a 300ZX.

One night after James and I went to bed, a call came from the Lake Jackson Police Department. I heard James say, "Officer, I will take care of it." Noel was out in the "crapola" car cruising around with three of his buddies. It seems that one of the boys threw a paintball out the back window at one of the paper distributors who was by the street preparing his papers for delivery. Rightfully so, it ticked the man off. He got the license number and reported the incident to the police. James waited, not too patiently, for the "cruisers" to return. He met them in the driveway. "Come on, boys." He piled them in the Suburban and carted them off to the police station. Upon arrival at the station, he sat them down in a

Noel and Amy – Belle dance

row of chairs. "Officer, they are all yours." This is the kind of father that James is and was. It turns out that Noel never knew that the paintball was thrown. The kid who threw it admitted as much. That kid never rode in the "crapola" car again.

J.T. often traveled with us. On one trip, we took him hunting at the ranch in Bandera which we leased for over forty years. He was a nice boy, and I was very attached to him. The first day J. T. went to the blind with me. We were in the blind for only a few minutes when the biggest axis I had ever seen walked out of the woods. When J. T. saw the deer, he whispered to me: "Mrs. Kyle, that's the biggest freaking deer that I've ever seen." After fighting buck fever, I shot the axis. He ran straight up the mountain. I told J. T. that we should wait in the blind for ten minutes before we could track it. After ten minutes, J. T. barreled out of the blind and started into the woods at the foot of the mountain. He found the axis a hundred yards up the mountain. Our axis was placed in The Record Book of Exotics and its head hangs on my wall today.

A few years ago, we purchased a small ranch in Junction, Texas, for hunting. Hunting in Texas has become an expensive hobby. Buying the ranch turned out to be a good idea. The Gordy's own the ranch next door and run longhorns on our place after hunting season is over. They are marvelous people and we love them dearly. We are fond of our little ranch and there is no shortage of deer and wildlife there. Last year, on a game camera, we picked up the image of a mountain lion watering near my blind. I don't walk well after my recent accident and back surgery. This is not the only reason I will be delivered to my blind. In past years, I walked.

During the many years that we hunted in Bandera, we were fortunate to have the company of our friends, Lee and Shirley Hartless. Shirley and I spent many hours looking for antiques while James and Lee hunted. Shirley is a fun person, and we had a ball. One day, we went into town for groceries, forgetting that this was the day of the cattle drive through Bandera. When we arrived in town, we blended into what we thought was the parade accompanying the cattle drive. Shirley was waving at everyone as we drove down Main Street. When the cars turned right at the red light, we realized we were in a funeral procession.

21

Golf and Sportscards

At some point, James and I started playing golf. Most of the time, we took Amy and Noel along. We soon noticed that Amy had an aptitude for golf. She joined the girl's golf team at Brazoswood High School and soon became the number one player. Larry Monte was the pro at our country club at that time, and his daughter Meredith was Amy's close friend. Larry took Amy under his wing for which we will be eternally grateful. Amy won the Houston Junior Tour Golf Championship when she was a freshman. It rained the entire tournament. Larry followed Amy around that Woodlands course, drying her clubs at every hole. He got soaking wet. Eventually, our daughter went to college on a golf scholarship. Since Mary Hardin Baylor is a rather expensive private school, this really helped out. The team went to the NAIA National championship tournament every year Amy was there. A year or two after Amy graduated the team won the NAIA National Championship. Coach Darla Kirby led the team to unprecedented success and is now an Associate Athletic Director at Mary Hardin Baylor.

Elementary school was a challenge for Noel. We went back to Bess Brannen Elementary many afternoons to find those lost papers mentioned in the teacher notes. Our boy always brought the notes home. He simply could not locate the papers. When Noel hit ninth grade, everything changed. By that time, I had opened an upscale antique shop on Flag Lake Drive. Noel began selling baseball cards in a room in the back. In order to get to Noel's shop, customers had to enter through mine. If Noel was late coming from school, kids would wait on a Victorian Love Seat that sat by the door. If the love seat was full, the kids would find another piece of antique furniture. Happily, there was an outside door leading into Noel's shop. We locked the doors that led from my shop into Noel's. Noel quickly had an outside entrance, and my antique shop was spared.

Noel's vocational education teacher, Roger Hammons, owned a jewelry store on Dixie Drive. Roger's store was directly in front of Noel's baseball card shop. Roger could supervise Noel directly. This allowed Noel to run his own shop, rather than work for someone else. Roger was an important role model in Noel's life. For his entire high school career, Noel tended his little shop. He became factory direct with most major card companies. Experiences provided by the card shop were vast. We spent a week in Atlanta at the National Card Collector's convention. Noel collected hundreds of autographs of famous sports figures. He also met many stars, including Mickey Mantle and Shaquille O'Neal. Prior to the convention, he commissioned Mickey Mantle to sign three baseballs. He bought baseballs by the case for signings and for sale to others for signings. Mantle signed two balls for Noel. I asked him to autograph the third to Chuck Barefield, who was a Mantle fan. At that time, Chuck was ill. Mantle, in a gruff voice muttered, "I don't do that." I never cared for Mickey Mantle after that.

During Noel's junior year, we traveled to Corpus Christi for a signing with Emmitt Smith. Amy had played a tournament two summers in a row in Pensacola, Florida. It was played on Smith's home golf course. Pensacola was his home town. Noel had prepaid for several items to be autographed, including an expensive helmet. We had been told not to speak to Smith so as not to hold up the line. When I got to him, I simply could not resist. I said to him: "My daughter has played your golf course in Pensacola several times." He broke out into a big smile.

The first summer we were in Pensacola for the golf tournament, we took extra time to vacation. Before the tournament began, we spent two days snorkeling on the Western end of Santa Rosa Island. The first day went great. The second day, I put sun screen on everyone except myself. I spent all day snorkeling with my back out of the water. By the time we got back to the room, I realized that I was burned more severely than I had ever been before in my life. I could not stand for anything to touch my back, and I could not put a shirt on. I had the print of that burn on my body for years. I cried from the pain and also because I missed seeing my daughter play golf.

Amy had many exciting experiences as a result of her golfing. Members of the Houston Junior Golf Association were asked to caddy at the Pro Am held before the Shell Houston Open each year. Her senior year, the gentleman she caddied for was paired with Payne Stewart. He was concerned that Amy was carrying his large, heavy bag and continually expressed it. During play, Payne handed Amy his club. "Amy, hit it across the water for me." Amy was so shook-up that she refused to do so. After the golf game was over, he gave Amy several of his specially marked balls and told her to stand by him while he did an in-

Amy at Riverside

terview on Channel 2. After the interview, he promised to give her some autographed pictures. As the interview closes, you can hear him speak to Amy: "Come on, let's go get those autographed pictures." James and I paid Channel 2 fifty dollars for a copy of that tape. The story is not over. The next year, two weeks before the Houston Shell Open, our telephone rang. I was shocked to hear a voice say. "Mrs. Kyle, this is man for whom Amy caddied in last year's Pro Am." He went on to tell me that he had arranged for

Amy to caddy for him again. He also said that he had purchased a new, smaller bag for her to carry. What a nice man! It broke my heart to tell him that Amy was in college in Tulsa and could not caddy for him. We have a picture of him with Amy; however, we have no idea who he was. I'm sure we knew at one time. There has been too much water under the bridge. He was definitely someone important or he would not have been playing in that tournament!

Amy and Payne Stewart

The next year Amy met Payne Stewart again in Tulsa where she was attending Oral Roberts on a golf scholarship. (After her freshman year, Amy transferred to Mary Hardin Baylor.) The girls' golf team was assigned to ferry players during the PGA Championship Tournament at Southern Hills. Payne Stewart remembered Amy and was very kind. He actually invited her and other members of the golf team to a party one evening. He told her that the PGA was entertaining some college-age male golfers from England, and it would be nice for them to meet some girls their own age. Amy said the food spread was fabulous. Apparently, the girls were more interested in the food than the English golfers!

Noel went to Mary Hardin Baylor as a sophomore. He took college courses while in high school as part of a program started by the school district and Brazosport College. His freshman year he ran for class president at Mary Hardin Baylor, only to come in second. Later he said, "Mom, anybody who runs for class president at a college where the ratio of boys to girls is one in four, is not too smart." I am happy to report that Noel is very successful and very smart.

22

Assorted Things

My friend, Sandra Lea, has informed me that I cannot write this book without mentioning the TECAT. The TECAT was designed to raise public confidence in Texas teachers by weeding out incompetence. What it did was make 210,000 teachers go ballistic. All degreed Texas Educators were required to take it in March, 1986. It seemed clear that failure to pass this test would result in eventual dismissal. We prepared before school, after school and at home, in small groups and large groups. Anxiety increased as the test date approached. Ninety-nine percent of the two hundred ten thousand who took the TECAT passed it. This didn't help Governor Mark White in his bid to win a second term. Teachers got a pass-fail score. We never knew what we actually made. I choose to believe that most of my friends made a perfect score. I convinced James that I did.

Mary Florence Platt, another good friend, tries her best to keep me in line, mostly to no avail. A year or two ago, my cousin, John Farr's daughter, Sarah, got married in a lavish wedding in New Orleans. I knew that my sweat pants were inappropriate. Mary Florence decided that we should go to Nordstrom in Houston to increase my wardrobe. I have never liked to shop. Mary Florence loves it! She arranged for a personal shopper and off we went. When we arrived, we were taken to a large fitting room with several mirrors. The room was already filled with outfits. As I tried on various things, I stopped asking how much. Toward the end, the personal shopper brought out a pair of handmade, Italian shoes. I was told that there was good news and bad news. The good news was that the shoes matched most of my outfits. The bad news is that the price was four hundred fifty dollars. Why I bought those shoes, I'll never know. I normally don't pay that much for anything but an antique. I was more than ready to check out with my expensive purchases. I gave the lady my credit card. It was declined. You should have seen the look on Mary Florence's face! I was hot! I pulled out another credit card which thankfully, went through. When we got home, I called the credit card company to find out why my credit card was declined. They had called my home in Lake Jackson to verify that the purchase was mine. When I didn't answer, they were afraid that my card was stolen and declined it. They also added that it was an unusually large purchase. No kidding! Now, I know why they make cell phones. A credit card company can't reach you at home on your land-line when you are not there.

When we arrived at the Royal Orleans in New Orleans for the wedding, we had a wonderful surprise when we reached our room. There was a gorgeous arrangement of flowers sitting on the table. Who would do this? Mary Florence, of course.

23

On The Road Again

When Amy was in sixth grade, we took her to Europe. On this trip I had my own epiphany. Gloria Faye, you aren't the only one. I was standing in the Louvre Museum in Paris staring transfixed at the Mona Lisa. Tears began to stream down my cheeks. My emotions erupted. Amy asked, "Mama, what's the matter?" I replied, "Baby, I can't believe I'm standing in front of the Mona Lisa." At this moment, I realized I had discovered a larger world. At eleven, Amy did not understand the significance of my standing in front of the Mona Lisa.

Amy was fascinated by Reba Macintyre. In 1991, we took Amy and Noel to Fan Fair in Nashville. If you love country music, it is an experience of a lifetime. Fans get to meet big stars face to face, and we met them all. Clint Black, Charlie Pride, Ricky Van Shelton, Loretta Lynn, and Ricky Skaggs are some that I remember. Amy was a Reba fan club member. We were invited to a private party that Reba gave at the Municipal Auditorium in Nashville. Crook and Chase were taping. I have no idea how Amy and Noel got before the camera, but they did. The next day, their Grandmother Stoker caught them on the Nashville Network. She was thrilled. Reba posed for pictures with all of us.

Another funny incident happened. I had to go to the restroom. I wandered down this long hall that surrounded the auditorium and finally found the restroom. I opened the door, and suddenly someone flew by me and ran into a stall. I knew it was

Reba and James – Nashville

Reba because she was wearing a black leather outfit that she had just worn in a movie she was making. Another epiphany, celebrities have to pee, too.

Since Amy was so crazy about Reba in those days, we saw her pretty often. We always got to go backstage after the concerts because of the fan club. On one occasion, a publicity person brought in a Reba look-a-like. She really did look like Reba; however, it made Reba livid for some reason. The impersonator was whisked out of there really fast. Amy has a stack of Reba pictures and autographs somewhere. As I was pouring through items in preparation for this book, I found two pictures that Reba had autographed for me.

When we were at Fan Fair, Charlie Pride was staying in the same hotel. When Noel was getting his autograph, he just had to tell Charlie that we were in the same hotel. Charlie said, "Please don't tell anyone where I'm staying because fans will wart me to death." Noel promised. He never said a word and neither did we.

James took me to New England on a buying trip. We have been fortunate to travel many places. For me, these three weeks were one of the best things that James had done for me. Antiques are my passion. I love buying and selling them. I think I'm pretty good at it. We flew to Boston, rented a car and hit the back roads. I had previously shopped in Pennsylvania; however, New England was an antique dealer's dream. I took packaging in my luggage and we collected boxes along the way. After shopping all day, we boxed up the purchases at night. The first thing each morning, we located the nearest UPS Store. I more than paid for the trip with my finds. A funny thing happened at one of the UPS stops. The clerk asked us if we were Q Tips. Puzzled, I asked him what he meant. He responded that the New Englanders called the tourists who came up to see the fall foliage, Q Tips. I still did not get it. Realizing this, he said, "Those buses are everywhere and all you can see is those little gray heads. They look like Q Tips." Live and learn.

I love lobster. I ate so much on that trip that it's a wonder that I didn't start to crawl. We ate at some fabulous restaurants and stayed at neat places. Nothing surpassed the buying opportunities, however.

On one trip to Key West, we went on a snorkeling trip on

Thinking about a new career in Rhode Island

Captain Amy – Key West

a big catamaran. I didn't go in the water and was watching the snorkelers from the deck. I saw Amy swim into a school of fish. I watched helplessly as she was joined by a six-foot shark. She saw the shark out of the corner of her eye and made a quick exit. It scared me to death. On this same trip, I watched a man almost drown. He appeared to be a non-English speaking tourist with no snorkeling experience. From my perch on deck, I saw him struggling and screamed to the captain. By this time, the other swimmers had noticed him. They called to the man to take his snorkel out. He did not understand because of the language barrier. One of the crew, a female, dived in and saved him. The captain let Amy drive the boat part way back. We have pictures to prove this. He was a cutie and evidently though Amy was, too.

On this same trip, we had one of the finest culinary experiences of our lives. Latitudes is a beautiful restaurant located on a tiny mangrove island about ten minutes from Key West by boat. This is the place to view the sunset. Noel, Amy, and my grandchildren were with us this trip. We dined

Logan and Riley, our grandchildren, at Latitudes

on seafood adorned with fresh tropical fruit in this breathtaking setting. I remember how cute Riley and Logan looked sitting in the Ernest Hemingway room acting like big people. Hopefully, Latitudes survived Hurricane Irma.

We have been blessed to visit many beautiful places, none more beautiful than the British Virgin Islands. The islands were not cluttered with tourists, and we freely drove a rented jeep around the big island. We took ferries and hailed boats to get to the other islands. We were told about Smuggler's Cove where the second *Old Man and the Sea* was filmed. We found it and snorkeled there several afternoons. We were often the only ones there. James had trouble staying on the correct side of the road. A few close calls ensued. We hired a couple of guys to take us by boat to Jost Van Dyke. We probably didn't need to get in the boat with these fellows. They looked like left-over pirates. Jost Van Dyke is a small Island which houses White Bay Beach. This beach was named one

Above **Noel, Riley and Logan snorkeling off Key West**

Below **Riley and Logan having fun**

Amy and Noel – Key West

of the most beautiful beaches in the world by *Conde Nast Magazine*. We also frequented Foxy's Beach Bar, a Kenny Chesney hangout. Amy loves Kenny Chesney and actually named her Pomeranian Chesney. These beautiful islands have been decimated by Irma. Recent reports indicate that the physical building that

Above **James in his Foxy's t-shirt**

Right **Amy and Foxy – British Virgin Islands**

was Foxy's is gone. A secondhand report thankfully indicates that Foxy and his family are safe. One afternoon, Amy visited with Foxy for an hour. The bar was empty and he was not busy. He played and sang for her. I appreciated that he took that much time to speak with her. James still wears his Foxy's muscle shirt.

Another of our more recent travels was a trip to Cabo San Lucas, Mexico, to fish for striped marlin. Amy caught a trophy striped marlin after fighting it for an hour. The boat captain told her that it would have been an eighty-five thousand dollar

fish if she had been tournament fishing. James and I had a replica made which hangs on her wall today. This trip is ingrained in my mind for another reason. As we touched down on the runway at Los Cabos Airport, it seemed that the pilot lost control. I had accumulated enough air miles to know that this was serious. The plane bounced from side to side with the wings nearly touching the runway each time. It was not the conventional bad landing. I really felt that we were going to crash. Thankfully, the pilot got the plane under control, and we came to a stop at the end of the runway. Even James was shaken. The young lady in the seat next to me looked me in the face and confided, "I think I've peed in my pants."

On a business trip to Europe, Amy and I were left with time on our hands since James had several work days in Terneuzen, The Netherlands. Our former neighbors, Cathy and Irby Jones, were on Dow assignment there. Cathy and I were business partners at one time. During the same time frame, Irby's mother and a friend were visiting them from Alabama. Cathy had plans to take them to London. Amy and I were able to tag along. We drove to Calais, France, where we took a hovercraft to Dover, England. When the White Cliffs of Dover appeared in the distance, I was reminded of the World War ll story told by British and American pilots.

Becky and James – British Virgin Islands

As they returned from bombing missions in Germany, often with damaged planes, they felt home free when they saw the cliffs. The song, "*White Cliffs of Dover*" was very popular during the war.

Our reservations were at the Grosvenor Hotel in London. Upon arrival, we found that a problem existed with Cathy's two rooms. Amy and I were hungry. We decided to have lunch while Cathy was dealing with the room situation. We located the hotel restaurant and sat down to order. Our tourist attire did not attract a waiter since everyone else was dressed to the hilt. Women wore hats and gloves and the men wore top hats and long jackets. Finally, it dawned on me that this was the day of Royal Ascot. I don't remember if we ever got served.

We toured London the next day. The evening of the second day, we had tickets for *Starlight Express*, a Broadway musical which was then in a London theater. Like any Andrew Lloyd Webber production, the musical was wonderful. After thirty plus years, it returned to London in 2017. When we exited the theater, I tried unsuccessfully to hail a cab. The theater district went dark, and I was still trying to get a cab to stop. Finally, one stopped. The cab driver told me that he could not take all six of us. I knew that I could not leave anyone alone in this situation. My solution was to tell the driver that I was prepared to give him the biggest tip that he had received in a while. We got into the cab. Amy and Cathy's daughter, Patty, knelt on the floorboard on the ride to the Grosvenor. We were dropped off in the shadows, about a block from the hotel. I tipped the cab driver one hundred American dollars. Thirty years ago, that was a lot of money.

James met us the next day. After touring London for two or three more days, we returned to Calais, where James had left the rental car. I remember buying the most beautiful set of sterling fish knives in London. I kept them several years. Eventually, I sold them for a nice price. When we have dinner guests, James enjoys telling them, "Turn your plate over. It probably has a price tag on it."

Our next stop was Brugge, Belgium. We stayed in a lovely bed and breakfast which was filled with beautiful flowers. One evening, we went to dinner at a nice restaurant on the town square. The air was filled with excitement, and all kinds of things were going on. James did not realize that the waiter had not given his credit card back until the next day when we started to check out of the bed and breakfast. We went back to the restaurant to retrieve the card. The waiter denied that he had failed to give the card back. Before we left Brugge for Amsterdam, we went by the police department to file a complaint. We were given a copy of the complaint document. This turned out to be a smart move. After we arrived home, so did our next Visa bill. On the bill was a forty-seven hundred dollar charge to the Bunny Club in Philippine, The Netherlands. Philippine is part of the municipality of Terneuzen. Because we had proof that this was a scam, Visa took care of the charge. James kept saying. "Thank God, you were with me on this trip."

24

More School Stories

My years in Brazosport Independent School District were rewarding and challenging. As I look back on my career, I have no regrets. I gave beyond the call of duty as did many of my colleagues. I was voted Teacher of the Year in both schools where I taught. I consider this a great honor. When technology was first introduced in the district, we were ill-equipped to deal with it. We were required to input our grades into a computer when our science wing only had four computers. Seven teachers and four computers! Not so good! Today, the technology program in the district is second to none.

During my tenure at Lake Jackson Intermediate School, I was pulled out of the classroom to teach the AID'S program. I, along with the guidance counselor and the school nurse were chosen for this gem. After months of curriculum development, we started the classes. Thank heavens the classes were segregated by sex. The last period of the day, we had the eighth grade boy's athletic class. This was basically the football team. Prevention was under my jurisdiction. I felt it necessary to hammer down hard on this particular group. In my discussion, I indicated that incorrect use of condoms could result in contacting the virus. This kid on the first row began waving his hand in the air, at which time, I called on him. His question was: "Mrs. Kyle, what do you mean by incorrect use of a condom?" Before I could answer, this big, burly kid sitting next to him slapped him on the back and said,

"Putting it on your toe, idiot." I lost it.

I transferred to Grady Rasco Middle School after twenty-eight years at Lake Jackson. I felt that a change would be good for me, and it was. My principal at Rasco, Sandy Antill, was a dream to work for. I value her friendship today. I was the only teacher there who had taught under Mr. Rasco.

Teacher of the Year presentation

Rasco had a bit of a snake problem, possibly because we had a fantastic natural area with a small pond. I was the snake lady because of my extensive biology background and probably also because everyone else was petrified of them. I removed more than a few non-poisonous snakes from the building. I took a day off, and of course, a little grass snake appeared." Sandy told me that I could not take any more days off. She was kidding. One day, this kid comes running into my classroom right in the middle of my lesson. She said, "Mrs. Kyle, come quick! There is a big snake on the deck in the nature center." Not so funny this time. I ran out to find a four-foot water moccasin sunning on the deck. A teacher saw it as she was taking her class into the area for a lesson. By the way, I could still run in 2000. I ran into the building and grabbed a hoe from the tool closet. By the time I returned, the snake had disappeared into the water. Sandy locked the gate on the nature center for the rest of the year.

25

Still Traveling

I planned to retire in 2000 so that I could travel with James for a year before he retired. James asked me what I wanted to do for my retirement present. I replied that I wanted to go on a fishing trip to Minnesota to fish for walleye. Immediately after school was out, we left for Minnesota to fish for walleye and muskies in Leech Lake near a town called Walker. The lodge was rustic and lovely. In the evenings, we built a fire on the beach, sat on logs and enjoyed the ambiance. Sitting on the logs reminded me of Aunt Ollie again. We caught plenty of walleye, but soon found how illusive muskies can be.

Half-way through the trip, we received a call from my cousin telling us that Daddy was ill. I can still picture James in a phone booth in the middle of nowhere, trying to make reservations from Minnesota to Baton Rouge. We arrived in Baton Rouge at some ungodly hour. Daddy was in an assisted living facility at this time. When I saw him, I knew instinctively that it was time to bring him to Lake Jackson. I hired a lady to stay with him twenty-four hours a day, until I could return. He had already made it clear that he did not want to live with us. James was able to get us on the Dow plane to fly back to Lake Jackson. When we arrived home, Joyce was waiting for us at the airport. She dropped James and our luggage off at our house. Joyce and I set out to find the right facility for Daddy. I knew it had to be a full-service nursing home.

We found the best place for Daddy. In two weeks, we had him

moved in. All of the residents and staff loved him. He taught a Sunday School Class in the years he was there. James would always bring him to the house for LSU football games. After a while, he would say, "I'm ready to go home."

James had also planned a six-week working trip to Europe in July after I retired. This was to be another of our dream trips. Daddy had just arrived in Lake Jackson. There was no way that I could leave him in a strange place for a month and a half. At this time, Amy was between semesters in college. James flew her to Europe for a week in my place. James told me numerous times that this trip felt like a lifetime. Today, I am sure the trip would have been full of laughter and togetherness, but I did the right thing.

I am reminded of a trip that James took Noel on when he was a freshman in high school. James had business at one of the Germany sites. They flew there first and then on to Barcelona, Spain. From Barcelona, they drove to the Dow site in Cambriles, Spain. The hotel in Cambriles was on the beach. James felt that Noel would be safe there on the beach while he was working. Cambriles, like many European beaches, is a topless beach. Noel had taken a year of high school Spanish, and he thought he was cool, that is, until he saw those top-less girls. James said. "Noel, when you go to the beach, ask one of those girls to put suntan lotion on you." James knew that Noel rubbed it on himself because he had hand prints all over his back where the suntan lotion had blocked the sun. When he got back from work and joined Noel at the beach, James could not help but laugh. When the topless girls ran to get under the beach shower, Noel would make a bee-line for the shower. Baby boy just wanted a closer look.

On that trip, Noel ate anything that was thrown at him. For example, he ate minnows and cigala, a crustacean that looks like a cross between shrimp and lobster. James said when the natives ordered something, Noel wanted to try it. The irony is that Noel got deathly ill on pizza in Brussels.

The family took a ski trip to Breckinridge, Colorado. We were concerned that the kids had not experienced snow skiing. I guess we thought they needed to experience everything. During spring break that year, we planned a skiing trip to Colorado. We loved the atmosphere of the ski resort, which was ski in, ski out. The bad part is that James and I didn't take to skiing too well. He did better than I did. Noel and Amy took to it pretty well. Being the athlete

I thought I was, I was having a fit. It seemed a good idea for me to take lessons. The instructor took me up a steep slope that eventually led to the parking lot. We worked on different things, and she decided that I was ready to ski. I finally stood up on the icy snow with her help. She let me go and for the life of me, I could not stop. All I could see was the drop off to the parking lot. I could not remember how she had taught me to stop. As I got nearer and nearer, I thought that my only alternative was to throw my ski poles down and hit the ground. If you remember when ABC introduced a sports program with "The thrill of victory and the agony of defeat," then you can identify with my situation. Leave out the "thrill of victory." I tumbled down the slope and stopped just before the drop-off to the parking lot. I landed facing the instructor up the slope: She shouted, "Are you okay"? My answer was unclear. I was bruised from head to toe. This ended my skiing career.

Since I realized that I was not destined to become an Olympic skier, I put my skis away and departed to the grill. When asked what I wanted, I said, "I want a hamburger with the onions cut." The kid served me my hamburger. It must have had a pound of slivered onions on it. I said: "Son, I told you to cut the onions." "Lady, I cut the onions the best I could," was his response. So much for ski resorts!

James has a good friend in Canada who also worked for Dow. He invited James to hunt and fish when he was in Canada on business. Ken provided James with some unforgettable wildlife experiences. On a trip with Ken Pylypchan, James missed the biggest deer he had ever seen. James was standing in knee-deep snow when he shot. He has told me many times that he was freezing to death. James seldom misses, so I know that he was cold.

Ken invited the family to go fishing after James had completed a Dow business trip to Edmonton. We booked into the West Edmonton Mall Hotel. At that time, West Edmonton Mall was the largest in the world. When we were checking in, the clerk was so taken with our Southern accent that she upgraded us to a theme suite. Naturally, James let the kids pick the suite. They picked the truck suite. It was unbelievable. The suite was huge. We had a private hot tub and other amazing amenities. The kids had neat beds placed in interesting areas. The biggest problem was our bed was in the back of a pick-up truck with a mirror above. Believe you me, I could not make this up. I made a trip or two to the bathroom

Noel – Lac La Biche Canada Pike

during the night. I confided to James that I would have a hard time explaining to my friends how I had fallen out of a pickup truck during the night and broken my leg. I managed to crawl out of the pickup safely during the night for my bathroom trips. What a waste of a mirror!

After James finished work, we drove to Lac La Biche, a large lake in north-central Alberta to meet Ken. We had reservations in the small town of Lac La Biche several miles from the Lake. The only thing that could be said about the hotel is that it offered the basic necessities. The telephone service was terrible. Ken warned us to watch out for the natives who would wonder into the road when they were inebriated. This was a definite problem as we drove back to our hotel after dark each evening. It was frightening.

Pylypchan camped at the lake while we stayed in town. We hung around his camp site when we were not fishing. I got friendly with the park rangers and was intrigued by their bear stories. I got less intrigued when I was told that the week before, a bear walked into the campsite where Pylypchan was camped. When the rangers found out that I was from Texas and a science teacher, they wanted to know everything about rattlesnakes. I laid it on thick although my experience with rattlesnakes was limited. After we bought the ranch in Junction, this changed. When James leaves for his deer blind, I always say, "Watch where you walk."

We caught a massive number of pike and enough walleye to feed us every evening. Walleye are the best tasting fish I have ever eaten. Our Alberta trip was great.

After our fishing adventure, we drove to Jasper National Park. We sidetracked through the Maligne Mountains to Lake Maligne. Except for White Beach, I've never seen a more breathtaking place than Lake Maligne. Two teen-agers fishing from a dock had the most beautiful creel I've ever seen. I offered them one hundred dollars for it. I felt really bad when they explained that it was their grand-father's. That drive took my breath away. We saw every type of wildlife imaginable. James got much too close to several bears, and I probably got too close to a few elk. When we got to Banff, we were expecting to play golf and we did. We found ourselves waiting on every hole for the

Becky – Lake Maligne Canada

elk to exit the green. On the drive to Banff, we experienced a snow storm. This was in the middle of summer! A group of kids on a bicycle trip got caught in the storm and were freezing to death. They built fires at a roadside area in an effort to stay warm. We felt sorry for them.

Becky and Amy – Mama's retirement party at Riverside

26

A Few Other Things

My retirement party was held at Riverside Country Club. The ballroom was filled with friends. It was hilarious. Several did imitations of me, including Sandy Antill. Chris Crainer brought the house down. The big surprise was that Amy spoke before that huge group. Her remarks got to me. When I spoke, I found myself walking around the room, making comments about each person there. Every woman in that room was special to me in some way. The last day of school was a workday, and I was honored again during the luncheon that we always had. I'm seldom at a loss for words. When Sandy handed the mike to me, I broke down and was never able to recover. All of a sudden, it hit me that I was giving up one of the most important parts of my life. Later on in the day, I received a dozen red roses from James with a card that read: "Today is the first day of the rest of your life."

In 2013, James and I were finalists for Brazoria County Citizen of the Year. Both of us felt that others deserved it more. Over the years, we have done our best to serve our community both financially and through service. As a community service, I give free advice to families needing help with estate settlement. I do not do estate sales; although I have done free appraisals for families with limited financial assets. Earlier, James worked with the city to improve drainage on our block. Our drainage problem was greatly improved by his efforts. Today, James is the neighborhood watch chairman. His duties take many forms. He takes care

Above **Logan, Cory, Noel and Riley**

Below **Noel and Cory – on vacation**

of anyone who needs his help.

Our son Noel's first marriage produced two beautiful children, our grandchildren, Riley and Logan. Noel's present wife Cory is an accomplished young woman who has become an unbelievable mother to his children. Cory earned a Master's in finance and is a real helpmate to our son. Not long ago, Noel said to me, "Mom, I always hoped that I could find someone to love me. I never dreamed that I could find someone who loves my children like Cory does." Both Noel and Cory are successful. They have a beautiful home in Plano and live a rather charmed life. They are able to travel extensively. Each year, they take the kids on a special "kid's

trip". At this time, Noel flies to Seattle every other week for work. This is tough on them.

Vestie Helm worked for us for over forty years. It was a sad day when she could no longer work. Vestie was part of the family and we all love her. With the help of Mary Florence, we found a darling lady, Zita Mata. It has not taken long for her to blend into our family. James is as protective of Zita as he was of Vestie. At this time, James and I are finally rid of a respiratory infection that was awful. He was so worried about Zita catching it that he texted her and gave her the option of not coming to work. The next thing I knew, he was in the bedroom changing the bed covers. "What are you doing?" I asked. He informed me that the sheets and pillowcases were full of germs and that he did not want Zita handling them. What a guy!

After retirement, James seemed really pleased he did not have to get dressed each day for work. Most days, at work, it was business casual. At one point, he was flying to Austin each day to deal with an environmental problem. This necessitated a suit. As he transitioned into retirement, I noticed that he began to look really tacky. We started to town one day and I said, "I'm not going with you looking like that." Even today, it is difficult for me to go to town without seeing someone I know. Having lived in this town for fifty plus years and having taught over five thousand kids, it is almost impossible not to run into a friend, a parent or a former student. Reluctantly, James changed clothes. This inclination toward being tacky continues.

When James is dressed, he looks like a million dollars, at least to me. I have made sure that he has a nice wardrobe with everything matched and a fair share of designer shirts. It is a mystery how he can find the outfits he puts together. One day he walked out in a pair of cut-off shorts, a stained shirt and flip flops. Again, I refused to go with him to town. I looked him in the eye. "James, you have gone from Ralph Lauren to Billy Bob." I love him tacky and all.

27

The Old House and Barn

The farm in Ft. Jessup, Louisiana, is very special to us. Our grandchildren will be the seventh generation of our family to own this property. My great-grandfather settled it in 1818. My dad covered family history in his book, *Telling it Like it Was*, so I will leave most of this to him. In the seventies, Daddy gifted the property to us. James and I farm timber on the back acreage. The front forty acres borders Louisiana Highway Six and houses our lake and the Old Stoker House, our second home. In 1976, I did the research required to place the house in the National Registry of Historical Places. Along with the old barn, it was placed in the Registry soon after.

To this day, we are not sure when the house was built. I do believe that the barn was built before the house. As best that I can determine, the house was built in 1848. The famous historian Frederick Law Olmsted documented his stay at The Stoker house in his acclaimed book, *A Texas Journey*. Knowing that Olmsted arrived in Texas in 1853, it is clear the old house was built before then. Olmsted described what my great-great grandmother served him on that night in 1853. He dined on pork, both salt and fresh, cold cornbread and boiled sweet potatoes. Olmsted also stated that he stayed in a lean-two behind the house that had a big fireplace in it. *A Texas Journey* gave me a wealth of information, including this revelation of a lean-to behind the big house. Today, there is no evidence that the lean-to ever existed.

Top **Old Stoker House late 1800's**

Bottom **Old Stoker House today**

In the summer of 2000, we donated the barn to the Rural Life Museum at LSU. The museum workers worked for days dismantling the old barn log by log. They numbered and color-coded each log. Unusable ones were marked and set aside. Each log was reassembled at the museum in Baton Rouge. Each rotted log was replaced. Today, the barn stands in a very prominent place in The Rural Life Museum. Every type of rural Louisiana architecture is represented there. The Stoker barn is an example of a double-pen barn, constructed of notched oak logs. The maintenance of a roof over the one hundred-fifty year old barn greatly improved its state of preservation. The tin roof was added in the 1920's and maintained thereafter by my grandfather, my father, and finally, my husband and I. If you go to Baton Rouge, please include the Rural Life Museum in your plans. It is well worth your time.

Stoker Barn circa 2000

The barn was dedicated with great fanfare. Many members of the family traveled to Baton Rouge for the festivities. I spoke, along with the Provost of LSU. As I began to speak, the cows and oxen that had been brought in to complement the barn began to moo and carry on. I was drowned out by these four-legged bovines. James taped my remarks. All you can hear is the animals. I thought my speech was pretty good. Evidently, they were not impressed.

If that old barn could talk, it would have some tales to tell. I remember that my Granny Stoker would take me to the barn with her. She would sit me up on a large corner post while she milked. It was here that I received my first lessons in English slang. When Dot, the milk cow, kicked Granny, a choice word usually came out. *Shit* was one of Granny's favorite words. It sounded neat to me. One day I used it in front of Mother. She had a fit and asked where I heard it. "Granny said it." Mother didn't say a word. I must confess that I've used it a few times since.

28

The Golden Girls

Carolyn, Joyce, Peggy Lee, and I are what you might call "best friends." Peggy left us a few weeks ago. We are heartbroken. Her kind, sweet spirit will be with us forever. Until my health and Peggy's health failed, we had lunch together at least once a week. We called ourselves the "Golden Girls." After the barn was donated, we invited the "Golden Girls" to Baton Rouge for "An Evening at Windrush." James and I purchased a table for this gala event which raises money for the Rural Life Museum. Windrush is a beautiful plantation home which sits on over four hundred acres given to LSU by the Burden family years ago. This valuable land sits in the heart of Baton Rouge and houses the Rural Life Museum also. Much of the other acreage is used for LSU's horticulture research. Strawberries, flowers and other plants grow in experimental rows. I remember seeing a bunch of little golf greens in one area. I guess that research was being done on "green" grasses. "An Evening at Windrush" takes one back to the plantation days in the Old South. It was an elegant party, catered at that time by famous Cajun chef John Folse. The girls were able to meet the President of LSU and Mrs. Paula Manship, who donated the thousands of dollars to move and restore our barn. Mrs. Manship owned *The Baton Rouge Advocate* and was a well-known philanthropist. Confession is good for the soul. We also hit the "boats" a few times on that little trip.

James later arranged a trip to Las Vegas for the four of us.

The Golden Girls: Becky, Peggy, Joyce and Carolyn

We stayed at Cesar's Palace; however we searched desperately for casinos with lower blackjack minimums. Celine Dion and Cirque du Soleil were on our agenda. We sat on the front row at Cirque du Soleil, not realizing that we would get soaking wet. I insisted that we see Wayne Newton. I just had to hear him sing 'Danke Schoen' one more time.

29

Restoring the Old Stoker House

You might be pleased to hear that I thought of the third reason why I love James. He has been willing to spend a considerable amount of money restoring the old house. When we first began the restoration, it was apparent that the house was sliding backward off the large rocks it stands on. A structural engineer was called in. We followed through by adding concrete piers under the house. Bring money!

The exterior of the house was in terrible shape. Wooden boards had been placed over the original logs. Many of them were rotten and needed replacing. The old dining room was separated from the kitchen by a wall. The wall was knocked out to make a larger, more useable kitchen. The oak, claw-foot dining table was purchased by my grandparents in 1897. We still eat some pretty fine meals around it. The house is full of American Oak pieces. All have been refinished. By the time, James and I inherited the house, everything inside was in a state of ill repair.

The open hall of the old dog-trot house was closed in around 1900. At the same time, my grandfather had one of the large bedrooms redone for Granny. It is characterized by carved designs around the ceiling, all done by hand. Originally, it was painted a Victorian blue color. The last painting was done during our restoration. We chose a subtle blue. It has become the sitting room, also housing two beds. It is known by the family as the blue room.

Mantle – the Old Stoker House

James spearheaded the restoration. He designed a large fireplace to replace the old, unusable one. Austin stone was purchased to be used for the fireplace front. I recall that we drove a hundred miles to Alexandria to pick it up for the brick mason. The back and forth, to and from Lake Jackson, during these months of restoration, was exhausting. In the middle of this fireplace ordeal, James wanted to go to Houston to buy some raw wood. I was puzzled. He found a place that sold raw wood from all over the world. We brought home a massive piece of mahogany. He had a beautiful mantle made for the fireplace out of that "tree." When the fireplace was complete, we made the trip to inspect it. James was unhappy with the size of the wood-burning area so he made the poor guy tear it out and start over. In the winter, we enjoy the fireplace beyond belief. Lloyd keeps plenty of good firewood cut.

A floor-length mantle covered the old fireplace. The finish had peeled. It was just plain ugly. When it was removed, I threw it in the "chuck it" pile. I kept looking at the old thing and finally concluded that I could not throw it away. We carted it back to Lake Jackson where I had it refinished. When I picked it up, I could not believe my eyes. The wood under the awful varnish was burled walnut and it was absolutely beautiful. We used it as a mock fireplace mantle in the dining area.

This year, we finished a second renovation. The old boards were soaking up paint by the gallon and every time we painted, it cost a bundle. James decided to cover the wood with heavy Hardy Board. It looks nice.

The Stoker House was placed in the National Register for several reasons; one being that it is the oldest house in Sabine Parish. Every year, Sabine Parish and Sabine County does a "sale on the trail." The old house sits on the trail or "El Camino Real." For the last two years, we have done the sale. We let other vendor's set up in the yard under the nice trees. All have a fantastic time. Interesting people come from all over Louisiana and Texas. The sale runs from San Augustine Texas to Natchitoches Louisiana.

Top **Carved Ceiling, Blue Room Old Stoker House**

Bottom **The lake, James' favorite place**

James and a Florida bass

My biggest problem is folks wanting to see the house. It bothers me that I have to decline; however, with us not in residence, I cannot afford to let people see the contents of the house.

One of the things about the farm that we particularly enjoy is the lake. We have stocked it with Florida bass, bream, and crappie. In the spring and fall, we catch nice strings of bass. It has not been long since I caught a five pounder off the dock. In the lake, we see water moccasins that could qualify for the *Guinness Book of Records*. One day, Lloyd and I were sitting on the front porch. James shows up on the four-wheeler with a big, live water moccasin dangling from a pitchfork. Lloyd took off like a duck after a June bug. After hearing a few choice words from his wife, James took care of the snake.

30

Friends and Loved Ones

My grandmother and Aunt Edna lived in the old farmhouse when I was growing up. After my granny died, Aunt Edna lived there alone for years. Some of my happiest days were spent at the old house. Granny was a worrier of the first degree. I fished in the pond and played in the woods. Whenever I wandered out of her sight, you could expect Granny to show up to check on me pretty quickly. In her later years, Aunt Edna was not well. Daddy, James and I hired a lady to stay with her until she passed away. She willed me her set of Fostoria and her set of sterling silver. I treasure both. More than that, she allowed her part of the farm to go back into the estate, eventually, giving James and me more property. Hopefully, she is looking down, knowing that we have done our best to preserve and care for this sacred family land. It should be noted that our property was part of an original land grant. I have the papers, signed in 1856 by President Rutherford B. Hayes. Attached to these papers is the Presidential Seal.

Jan and "Skeeter" Varnado are my Stoker cousins. They live three miles from the farm down a country road. Ironically, their daughter Jana married Donnie Smith, who is from Brazoria County. For years, Jan owned the Hitching Post in Many. It was recently sold after fifty years. "Skeeter", at ninety-one, is still a successful rancher and businessman. Jan was elected to the Sabine Parish Hall of Fame in 2010. She has received every honor that exists. James and I love them dearly and they form an integral part of our lives. Both look forward to our fish fries. Lloyd can fry some mean fish. "Skeeter" sits in the chair at the head of the table when we eat since he is the family patriarch. Our get-to-gathers are always loud and fun. They are the highlight of our trips to the farm.

It is sad that James and I have lost contact with friends from our early years. Roy Bush Bridges is a friend with whom we stay in contact. Roy was in our wedding and to this day, I can depend upon him for news from Pleasant Hill. Roy's dad owned the drugstore in town. His grandmother and aunt lived next door to us for years. Mother and Daddy loved Roy Bush and he loved them. The nursing home business has treated Roy well. He has been quite successful along with being great fun.

Roy Bush in his new tux and Mother

Roy bought a new tuxedo for our wedding. Other attendants rented theirs. I guess he just wanted a tux. Mother passed by him at the reception and said, "Roy Bush, I like your new tuxedo." Roy replied, "Mrs. Stoker, how did you know it was new?" Mother responded, "Because it still has the price tag on it." Gloria Faye reminded me of this goodie.

31

The Hunting Years

Today is November 4, 2017. For the first time in three years, I am sitting in my deer blind at our ranch near Junction, Texas. Months of physical therapy and perseverance have brought me to this place. The view from my blind is breath-taking. Two ridges, one higher than the other, can be seen in the distance. A road runs along one of the ridges. For years, I have watched a Junction school bus run that ridge to deliver kids at the end of the road. I never needed to check my watch. The bus always appeared at four thirty. Sadly, I will see the school bus no longer. The family at the end of the road has moved.

The smell of cedar is refreshing and invigorating. The air is clean and fresh. I had forgotten how serene this setting is. Two does have appeared at my feeder. I am practicing placing my rifle in a position against my shoulder which does not compromise my still tender incision. After satisfying myself that my incision is safe, I settled back down to making notes for this book. I looked up to see that a nice eight-point buck had joined the doe at the feeder. I shot and missed. Sick at heart, I recalled that this was only the second deer that I have missed in fifty years of hunting. I have killed many deer over the years. My text brought James to my rescue. I attempted to exit the blind before he arrived and found that he had locked me in the blind from the outside. I am very claustrophobic. It is a good thing that he arrived shortly after I discovered my dilemma! A day or two later, we saw the buck on one of our game cameras. Thankfully, I did miss him.

Our return to hunting has been a challenge. I had to figure out how to climb on the four-wheeler and into my blind. With the help of my husband, I was able to do both. I finally killed a nice eight-point and a doe for our housekeeper, Zita. James was also very successful. When we get home, our next trip will be to Snook, Texas. We have our deer sausage made there. We think it is the best in Texas.

James and I went on our first Texas deer hunt in 1970. Our little six-cylinder Ford pickup was loaded with guns, food and a mattress. We had plans to spend the night in the camper on the back of the pickup. After five hours, we arrived at the E.G. Pope Ranch in Helotes, Texas. We went inside the ranch house to register for the hunt. Clearly, Mr. Pope was surprised to see a twenty-something woman among the hunters. He found out that we were sleeping in the truck and would have no part of it. The "little lady", which is what he called me, and her hunting partner were invited to sleep inside the ranch house. We were also invited to have dinner with him. Our host barked orders to his Mexican staff as they prepared and served dinner. We dined on cabrito, beans, and tortillas.

After dinner, Mr. Pope conducted a drawing for doe tags. He had a basket filled with fake and valid doe tags. On the top, he had placed a real tag. He proclaimed, "The little lady will draw first." I reached in the basket and pulled out the valid doe tag.

Four o'clock the next morning came early. The temperature was twenty-five degrees. A pickup truck delivered us to the blind. By the time we exited the truck, we were freezing to death. The Mexican driver told us that he would be back at noon. After climbing into the blind, we huddled together to stay warm. As daylight dawned, it became clear that another hunter shared our sentiments. Above the blind window, the previous hunter had written: "I sat here all day, froze my ass off, and all I saw was two frigging blue jays." Our hunting trip ended at noon. James and I still laugh about this one. This was a far cry from the heated blinds that we enjoy today.

The next year, we decided to exchange day hunting for the Texas lease system. Our first lease was near Hallettsville, Texas. This was in 1970. I killed by first deer here. My spike buck was at least as big as a German shepherd. In 1972, we hunted in Camp

James with Becky and her axis

Wood, Texas, on the Woodward ranch. James built three blinds, one for me, one for Daddy and one for himself. One Friday in July, we started out for Camp Wood with the little Ford truck loaded to the hilt with the three disassembled blinds. In order to reach the lease, we had to cross a low-water bridge over the Nueces River. Upon arriving at the bridge, we saw that water was running over. James waded into the water and decided that we could make it across. By this time, it was midnight. I held my breath as we crossed the flowing water. I was never so happy to reach a dry caliche road. By the time we reached the lease, about seven miles up the road, we were dead tired. We pitched our tent, threw our sleeping bags inside and fell asleep immediately. Soon, we were awakened to headlights coming our way. We then heard a female voice. "You are in my camping spot." James hollered back. "I am not moving until in the morning."

It turns out that the voice was that of a retired teacher from

Houston. Gerry Powell turned out to be a piece of work. She had driven all the way from Houston, pulling an old jeep behind her pickup. We got to know her and found her entertaining and engaging. We never camped in her spot again!

For opening weekend, Daddy met us in Lake Jackson. The three of us drove to Camp Wood after school on Friday. We pitched our big tent, not designed to capture and hold heat. By this time, it was midnight and we were glad to get some sleep. At three o'clock, Daddy woke us up screaming. I thought he was having a heart attack. When I realized that his leg was cramping, I was so relieved that I belted him with my pillow. Daddy killed his first deer here, as did Mother. My first miss was here. Unfortunately, it was the biggest buck that I have ever seen in a low-fence setting.

The next year we leased a ranch in Bandera County, Texas, where the family hunted for forty plus years. After they retired, Mother and Daddy spent the entire month of November here. James and I came on weekends and Thanksgiving. Basically, we spent every anniversary in Bandera for forty years.

Amy and Noel made their first trip to Bandera when they were babies. Mother played with them and entertained them for hours upon end. One year, a small buck appeared at the camp fence. Amy fed him and he began to come back each evening. Mother wrote a precious story for Amy. She called it "Amy's Button Buck."

One November day, Mother and I were sitting around the fire pit visiting while Amy was playing inside the fenced camp. Suddenly, I missed Amy. Panic set in as Mother and I frantically searched for her. This went on for several minutes. Finally, I found her hiding behind the travel trailer wheel. She was playing hide-and-seek while Mother and I were terrified.

Noel killed his first deer in Bandera. He was about eight or nine. Over the years, he became a crack shot with both rifle and shotgun. I have seen him knock down doves that should have been out of range. As they got older, Amy and Noel often went to the blind together. One afternoon, when they were hunting together, I heard a shot which I knew came from Noel. Amy sent a text. "Noel got a nice one. He is dead in the water." James and I left our blinds to check out Noel's deer. Amy was correct. When Noel shot, the deer fell into the creek. He was dead in the water. Noel waded into the creek, tied a rope to the deer and pulled him out of the creek with the four-wheeler.

Over the years, Daddy and James disagreed over very little. One area of disagreement involved Daddy's safety consciousness. James would get livid when Daddy squirted charcoal starter from the can into an open fire. Daddy would say, "Jim, I have done this for years." He never changed his ways. One summer day, James and Daddy were clearing a road on the Bandera lease. James was cutting a limb while Daddy was pulling on it. James told Daddy to let go of the limb, which of course, he ignored. When the limb fell, so did Daddy, right into an agarita bush with its sharp, pointed leaves. Falling into an agarita bush is analogous to falling into a holly bush.

32

My Accident and Other Health Issues

In May of 2015, Lloyd was getting the boat ready for James and me to bass fish. He asked me to move the golf cart closer so that he would not have to carry the heavy trolling motor so far. I was sitting in the passenger seat. I reached across to move the cart forward. To this day, I do not know what happened. I ran the golf cart ten feet into the water at full speed. When it finally stopped and started to sink, I managed to get out. I took two strokes and realized that I could stand. I stood and sank into the mud. I ended up crawling most of the way out. I pulled myself onto the bank, looking as if I had been in a mud fight. James stood frozen during the entire ordeal. My ankle was cut and I felt a pain in my left leg.

At the time, I had no idea I was badly hurt. Lloyd hosed me off, and I actually walked the hundred yards up the hill to the house. It was unclear how badly I was hurt until we got home. My leg began to buckle under me, and I took two bad falls. After seeing a neuro-surgeon, I tried shots and physical therapy. One day, on the way to therapy, I took a nasty fall. I continued on to therapy. When my therapist looked at my leg, she told me that I did not need to do anymore therapy until we found out what was going on. James took me to Houston to another neuro-surgeon. The diagnosis was a compression in my back was causing me to lose use of my left leg. I was in the local hospital on the physical therapy floor for four weeks before the surgery and four weeks after. When we reported to Houston for my pre-op, the surgeon decided I was not in physical shape to undergo the surgery. I was sent back to our hospital for four weeks of therapy to build me up. I had the surgery and returned again for four weeks of in-hospital therapy. Afterwards, I was sent home for multiple weeks of in-home therapy. I worked hard and was doing well. I had progressed from being bed-ridden to walking without a cane. As I was walking through our den one day, the leg buckled. I fell on our coffee table and broke my shoulder bone in four places. As I write this, I continue to be in rehab for the shoulder.

Until I reached seventy, I had never had a knife in my body except when Dr. Prothro cut the Hula Popper out. After seventy, I have had two knee replacements, neck surgery, back surgery, and shoulder surgery. I have enough plates and screws in my body to be the bionic woman. Getting old is the pits! I surely cannot leave James out. He has endured prostate cancer surgery, hernia surgery, rotator cup surgery, varicose vein surgery, back surgery, and knee surgery. Another knee surgery is scheduled for December. The artificial knee is not working. The reason that we are waiting until December is that nothing interferes with hunting season, not even pain. Perhaps, no one is interested in our health issues; however, maybe this will get us a little sympathy. Thank the good Lord for insurance!

Some years ago, we had just pulled into the feed store in Junction when we received a call from James's urologist informing us that he had prostate cancer. We were buying deer corn for the ranch and suddenly found our lives turned upside-down. Dr. Goldfarb, James's urologist and friend, told us to finish hunting. We were to come see him in Houston. The solitary moments in my deer blind gave opportunity for me to imagine the worst and envision what life without James would be like. I could not come to grips with the possibility of losing him. We closed the blinds, sealed the cabins and headed home. We reported to Dr. Goldfarb for our appointment. He went through our options. I looked him in the eye. "Dr. Goldfarb, the only thing that matters is that you save my husband." Thank God, he did.

33

Grandma Kyle and Others

A few more people must be mentioned in these pages before I'm done. My mother-in-law, Frances Kyle, is one of these. She was wonderful to me. One of the many things that were great about her is that she never let me help her when James and I went to Monroe. It was a place where I could truly relax. On the way home from our wedding trip to Hot Springs, James and I spent the night in Monroe before heading to Luling. After visiting until late that evening, we went to bed. James got into bed first. When I crawled into bed, the bed fell in. It sounded like the roof had collapsed. (This happened when I was thin.) I have never been so embarrassed in my life because I knew what Mr. and Mrs. Kyle were thinking. We were totally innocent. I can hear Grandma Kyle now. "Henry, I told you to fix that bed." She was one of a kind. In later years, we had a motto: "Don't say no to Grandma Kyle because you will be wasting your breath". I loved her dearly.

Suese Cook is a great friend as is her husband, Jimmy. I met Suese years ago when she volunteered at the nursing home. She and Daddy became very attached to each other. At night, Suese played cards or dominoes with Daddy or simply assisted him with things he needed done. This helped me so much. I was usually exhausted from my teaching day. When I visited after school, I never felt bad about leaving because I knew Suese was right behind me. When Dad passed away, Suese said to me, "I do not want to lose contact with the family." I replied, "That's not going to happen."

And it didn't. Suese and I have spent many hours together, rummaging through junk shops, estate sales and antique shops looking for that "sleeper". I believe that she is the only person who could out junk me! Unfortunately, our health situation has put a damper on our excursions.

Suese's husband Jimmy is a prince. If I called Jimmy at this moment, he would be here in a second. Jimmy was checking our house while we were at the deer lease. He noticed that the hot water heater had cratered. By the time we returned home, Jimmy had bought and installed a new water heater. He and Suese are blessed to have found each other. We are blessed to know them.

Imy and Walter Hoffman lived around the corner from us for almost fifty years. James checked on him almost every day for years after Imy's death. Walter recently passed away. Imy was my partner in The Collector's Gallery. She was smart and had a wonderful knowledge of antiques. We

Mother and Dad Kyle on their wedding day 1940

spent many happy hours together. One day, I began to realize that Imy was ill. She passed away because of the ravages of Alzheimer's. Imy and Walter's son, Grant, is a friend. I taught Grant in eighth grade. It is interesting how things change. Today, Grant calls me Becky. There was a time when he knew to call me "Mrs. Kyle." James is fond of Grant and they enjoy great times together. Grant's wife Gale is a superb gal.

Another friend with whom I share an interest in antiques is Jo Ann Hall. When she calls me, I never know where she is until I'm told. Most likely, it is in an antique shop in some small Texas town. Jo Ann picks for me. In antique speak, this means that she buys for the shop. Jo Ann gives new meaning to the song *On the Road Again*. She sends me a picture of an item with the price, and I say yes or no. I provide her with signed exemption certificates and a cover letter explaining her role.   Jo Ann is one of the most caring persons I have known. She is a devout Christian and spends her life helping others. Her friendship is another of my treasures.

I could not continue to operate my antique shop without the help of my friend, Cathy Spinks. Cathy owns the "11th Street Mercantile" in Bandera. I rent space from Cathy and her partner. She has helped maintain my shop during this period of declining health. We love our visits with Cathy and her husband, Brad. They have joined us at the farm and in Lake Jackson.

I cannot end this book without recognizing one more friend. She is smart, full of energy and one of the most caring people we have ever known. Although, she prefers not to be named in my memoirs, she knows who she is and how much she means to us. When I was ill for so long, she was by my side night after night, both in the hospital and at home. When James was so tired he could not function, this wonderful woman was there to relieve him. We will love her forever.

34

Winding Down

James and I purchased our headstones and had them placed in the family plot in Ft. Jessup Cemetery. As we walked into Sabine Monument, I caught a finished monument out of the corner of my eye. With closer scrutiny, I noted the inscription. It has resonated in my mind since that day. It read. "Life is not the dreams we dream, but rather, the choices we make." I have thought many times about how this applies to my own life. I have dreamed dreams. Many have been realized. For the most part, I have made good choices. These choices have allowed me to enjoy a life filled with love, laughter and fulfillment. No doubt, growing up in a small town provided me with many of the tools I needed to make these wise choices.

I never dreamed that we would get old. It has been difficult to watch James unable to do so many things that he once could do. I am grateful for every day we have together.

As my thoughts are winding down, I find myself doubting the wisdom of this undertaking. It has been cathartic for me. I only hope that it will be fun and interesting for others to read. It is my prayer that I have not offended anyone. I have most certainly found that bigger world as I traveled the road of life with my James, our kids and many wonderful friends. I have few regrets because I have lived life to the fullest and enjoyed adventures that few have been privileged to experience. When all is said and done, for the most part, I charted my own course. I guess you could say, "I did it my way."